HOW TO BEAT LOW-LIMIT 7-CARD STUD POKER

HOW TO BEAT LOW-LIMIT 7-CARD STUD POKER

PAUL KAMMEN

CARDOZA PUBLISHING

FIRST EDITION

Library of Congress Catalog Card No: 2003100598
ISBN:1-58042-105-9

Visit our new web site (www.cardozapub.com) or write us for a full list of Cardoza books, advanced and computer strategies.

CARDOZA PUBLISHING
P.O. Box 1500, Cooper Station, New York, NY 10276
Phone (800)577-WINS
email: cardozapub@aol.com
www.cardozapub.com

ABOUT THE AUTHOR

Paul Kammen is an avid 7-card stud poker player and an expert at low-limit stud games. He has played low-limit 7-card stud in numerous home games and in many casinos. Since he first started playing stud poker, Paul has developed his game and techniques to help him maximize his profits and enjoy the game even more. He greatly enjoys sharing his secrets to help others improve their game of low-limit 7-card stud poker.

ACKNOWLEDGEMENTS

Many people have given me support in making this book a reality, and it would be impossible to thank them all. Specifically, I would like to thank Jan Fisher, *Card Player* magazine columnist and cruise director, for all of her help over the past several years. I wrote Jan for advice after reading one of her columns, and I've enjoyed corresponding with her since then. Her pointers have helped me make huge strides in my game.

I would also like to thank my parents, Dennis and Mary, and my good friends Chris, Ryan, Jenny and Mark, for their support as I have worked on completing this book.

A big thank you also to Dana Smith, owner of CardSmith Publishing. Ms. Smith read my manuscript, and she was very helpful in assisting me in finding the right routes to take to get my work published.

Finally, I would like to thank the publisher, Avery Cardoza, for giving me the chance to write this book. It is an honor to be among the authors who write for his company, which publishes excellent gambling books and software.

TABLE OF CONTENTS

1. INTRODUCTION   **9**

2. THE GAME OF 7-CARD STUD   **13**
Hand Rankings • The Play • A Positive Attitude • Going on "Tilt" • Don't Be Intimidated! • Remembering Cards • Check Out Other Games • The Importance of Odds • Study Your Opponents • Betting Styles • The Bluff • The Buy-In

3. THIRD STREET   **35**
Trips • Big Pairs • Middle Pairs • Low Pairs • Flush Draws • Straight Draws • The Best of the Rest • Quick Quiz: Third Street

4. FOURTH STREET   **59**
Trips • Two Pair • Big Pairs • Middle and Small Pairs • Flush and Straight Draws • Fourth Street: A Summary • Quick Quiz: Fourth Street

5. FIFTH STREET   **91**
The Monster Hands • Playing a Full House • Completed Flushes & Straights • Trips • Two Pair • Pairs • The Drawing Hands • Fifth Street: A Summary • Quick Quiz: Fifth Street

6. SIXTH STREET 119
The Monster Hands • Completed Solid Hands (Straights or Better) • Trips and Two Pairs • Pairs • Drawing Hands • Sixth Street: A Summary • Quick Quiz: Sixth Street

7. SEVENTH STREET 139
Raising on Seventh Street • Calling on Seventh Street • Folding on Seventh Street • Quick Quiz: Seventh Street

8. FINAL THOUGHTS 153
Online Play • Check-Raising • Keep Records • Always Be Learning • Table Image, Etiquette & Attitude • A Word on Tells • "You'll Never Beat the Low Limits!" • Do's and Don't's • The Last Word

APPENDIX: THE ODDS 167

GLOSSARY 171

1

INTRODUCTION

If you are reading this book, you've decided to devote your time to playing one of the best forms of gambling there is: poker. Instead of wasting your time plunking quarter after quarter into a slot machine, or spending hour after hour at the blackjack tables, where you will gradually lose money in the long run, you've chosen to play a game where you, and not the house, have the edge. Congratulations.

Poker is unique among all types of gaming because the player is competing not against the house, but against other people. As a poker player, you also have the chance to combine skill with luck to give yourself an edge. Forms of gambling such as sports betting and horse betting also offer good opportunities, but they require you to rely on a team or a horse to win you money. In poker, your winning depends upon your own skill. Luck is always important – you need the right cards to fall – but, over time, it's solid play and experience that will make you a winner. Played well, poker will give you incredible opportunities. It's capitalizing on these opportunities that is difficult.

I had my first experience with poker when I was about five or six years of age. My grandfather taught me the game, and, in looking back on it, it seems to me that our game was probably fixed. Why do I feel that way? Maybe it's because I seemed to win every time we would play. Or maybe it's because I distinctly remember one hand in which I somehow got dealt four aces and a joker.

Needless to say, I was already hooked as a kid. Fast-forward ten years, and I've become best friends with a guy called Chris, who starts throwing occasional poker parties. When you're five, having fun is the best part of playing poker. By the time you've reached high school, you've become aware of another perk. It's called money. Our poker parties in high school were nothing as wild as the stuff you see in the poker movies. You wouldn't find us playing no-limit hold 'em for $10,000 pots.

I remember impressing everyone when I walked away with a "massive" $30 pot after getting lucky on a game of "in-between." Thirty dollars may not be a lot of money to the guys at the $30/60 tables, but when you're in high school, it definitely qualifies you as a high-roller. None of us got rich from our parties, but we did have a good time, and it sure was nice when you could go home with a few more bucks than you came with.

A few years after I graduated, our state legislature finally gave the green light for a card room to be built at the racetrack near my house. The card parties were no longer an option, and I still had a great love for poker. I figured that stud poker sounded like fun, so I'd give it shot. I went down to the track's card room for one afternoon and found that I could hold my own. It was a great atmosphere, full of friendly players, and I left with more than I started with. Even though I won, what I remember most from that session was a loss: a beautiful jack-high flush I had was beat by an ace-high flush whose owner had pulled the ace on his last card (otherwise known as **the river**.) From that moment on, I tried to get back to the card club as much as possible.

Having a good first-time experience in a public card room was a great beginning, but I knew I needed to know more about the game. I started reading books on poker. Material on my game of choice, stud, was rather sparse, but I did find one good book. I also picked up some great poker literature on other games such as Texas hold 'em. I play whenever I can, be it at the card club or in a home game. When I'm not playing, I read about poker in books, in magazines, or on the Internet.

Reading that testimony, you're probably thinking one of two things. Either you're thinking, "Boy, this guy needs a life!" or you're asking yourself if I'm trying to become a professional poker player. Poker never has been and never will be my full-time job. I spend my summers working, and during the rest of the year I'm studying to become a Catholic priest (yes, that's true). But I happen to love poker, and as I've played it more, I've become a solid low-limit player. Some guys enjoy plopping down fifty bucks to play golf in an afternoon. Me, I prefer to spend my free time at the low-limit stud tables.

So, why write a book? In my years of experience with poker, I've been able to become a good player and a consistent winner. I have some good things to say about the game. I see many players who love stud poker as I do, are primarily low-limit players, and seem to make the same common mistakes again and again. I figured these folks could use a few pointers.

This book won't get you to the final table of Binion's World Series of Poker. It may not even do you much good at the $30/60 stud tables. What it will do is help you to become familiar with the wonderful game that is seven-card stud. I wrote it primarily for people who, like me, are perfectly content to play the low-limit tables because they find them affordable and comfortable.

If you haven't played in a public card room before and are considering going, or if you're a little in the dark about when to bet, call, raise, and fold, I hope that my book will be of some assistance. Maybe you're a regular home game stud poker player looking for a little help in improving. Hoping to beat your buddies in next Saturday night's game? This book will help you out.

2

THE GAME OF 7-CARD STUD

Like many players, the first time I sat down in a public card room, I was both nervous and anxious. I was nervous to be playing at the table for the first time, but also anxious to take a seat and get those chips. Fortunately, I didn't lose too much money at my first public game, but the way I played, I very well could have. I'd learned a few things about stud poker, but I knew very little about how to play and what to bet. Don't make the same mistake I did. Before you head to the card club, or even to the next game with your friends, learn the following important basics of stud poker play.

Hand Rankings

Which one is higher: a straight or a flush? Does a diamond flush beat a spade flush? If you have to think about these questions for even two seconds, don't sit down at the poker table before you've read this section. Following is a brief description of each hand, from lowest to highest:

High Card: Simply the highest single card. A deuce is the lowest card, and an ace is the highest card in the deck.

Pair: Any two cards of the same rank, such as 3 3.

Three-of-a-Kind (Trips): Any three cards of the same rank.

Straight: Any five, unsuited cards in a sequence, such as 4 5 6 7 8.

Flush: Any five cards of the same suit – clubs, diamonds, hearts or spades.

Full House: A hand with a three-of-a-kind and a pair to go with it, such as three aces and two kings.

Four-of-a-Kind (Quads): Any four cards of the same rank.

Straight Flush: Five suited cards in a sequence, such as the 4 5 6 7 8 of hearts.

Royal Flush: The five highest-ranking cards suited and in order: T J Q K A. A royal flush is the best hand in poker.

When two hands are the same (when both you and your opponent have a flush, for example) you do *not* split the pot. The winner in such a case is determined by rank of cards. Let's say you have a straight of 7 8 9 T J, and your opponent has a straight of T J Q K A. He wins, because his straight is to a higher card than yours. When two players hold a full house, the rank of the three like cards determines the winner. For example, let's say you hold 4 4

THE GAME OF 7-CARD STUD

4 A A, and your opponent holds K K K Q Q. Because his three kings are higher than your three fours, he wins.

The Play

If you've never played in a public card room before, the play of a hand can be confusing. Although different rules abound in home games, public card rooms and casinos follow set rules for the play of a hand. What follows is a brief description of what you should expect when you join a seven-card stud game.

When you first arrive at the table, you must "buy in" to the game. If you don't yet have chips, you purchase them from the dealer. There are two possible betting structures for a poker game. In a structured-limit game, there is a small amount and a big amount – $2 and $4, for example. As we'll see in later sections, specific rules govern when you can bet each amount. In a spread-limit game, the house establishes a range of amounts – $1-$5, for example – and you can bet or raise in increments of any amount within the range. If the game you've joined is a structured-limit game, you must "ante" or pay a small amount to join. If it is a spread-limit game, an ante may or may not be required for you to receive cards.

Five rounds of betting take place in 7-card stud, and between each you are dealt one more card. The betting will vary depending on the type of game. In a structured-limit game, betting will be in set limits; in a spread-limit game, betting can be between two amounts at any point in play of the hand.

When the hand begins, you will be dealt three cards. We're now in the first round of betting, also called **third street**. Two will be face-down (your **hole cards**), and one will be face-up (your **door card**).

In most structured-limit games, on third street, the player with the lowest exposed (door) card must bring in the betting for half of the small amount. For instance, in a $2/4 game, the holder of the low door card must bet a dollar. If he so desires, though, a player can bet the full amount (i.e. two dollars). From this point on, play progresses around the table to the left of the initial bettor. Players can either fold, call (match the bet), or raise.

While on third street, raises in a structured-limit game can occur only in increments of the small amount. Generally, a maximum of three raises is allowed before the pot is "capped," though it's rare that the pot is raised that high on third street. In the example of a $2/4 game, one player could raise the pot to two dollars, the next could raise it to four dollars, and the next player could raise it to six dollars. At that point, no further raises would be permitted until the next round of betting.

When there are two low cards of the same rank on the board (such as two deuces), the suit of the cards determines who is forced to bring in the betting. The suits are ranked in alphabetical order – clubs, diamonds, hearts and spades. The smallest possible card, then, is the two of clubs. Thus, if the two of clubs and the two of diamonds are on the board, the holder of the two of clubs must bring in the betting. Third street is the only round during the play of a hand where the holder of the low card starts the betting. In subsequent rounds, the player with the highest hand on the board begins the betting.

If you decide to stay in, you receive another card face-up. Now we're in the second round of betting, also called **fourth street**. In a structured-limit game, unless there is a pair on the board, betting again can occur only in increments of the small amount. In a $2/4 game, then, when it was your turn to bet, you could either bet two dollars or raise two dollars – but not four.

If there is an exposed pair, however, you have the option of betting or raising in increments of the big amount. The pair need not belong to you. For instance, let's say you have a pair of 5s on the board and what appears to be the highest hand at the table. You can bet either two or four dollars. Alternatively, let's say someone else has a pair and brings it in for two dollars. You can now raise either two or four dollars, making the bet four or six dollars to the next player.

If you again stay in, you receive a fifth card dealt face-up. You're now on **fifth street**. At this point, you no longer have the option of betting the small amount in a struc-tured-limit game. All betting from here on must be in increments of the high amount. Again, the high hand on the board initiates the betting, and again, a maximum of three raises is the rule at most card rooms. In fifth street play, then, a four-dollar bet could be raised to eight dollars, then raised to twelve dollars, and finally raised to sixteen dollars before being "capped." The sixth card is also dealt face-up, and play in that round (**sixth street**) works similarly.

The seventh card is dealt face down. You're now in the final round, called **seventh street**. Because there is no visible change to the hands, the highest ranking hand at sixth street again has the option to bet first. Play continues to the left until every player has chosen to fold, call, or raise. No more cards are dealt, and the remaining players in the pot either turn over their cards to expose their entire hands or **muck** (concede) the hand if they believe they are beaten.

If you're still in to call the last bet, always turn your hand over completely. Card rooms have a policy that "cards speak," which means that the dealer must see everyone's hand and declare the winner. You may very well have a hand you did not notice and end up winning the pot!

A Positive Attitude

Now that you understand the proceedings of seven-card stud play, a word about emotions and behavior at the poker table. Anytime you sit down at a poker game, you should be playing with the proper attitude. Noted author and professional card player Roy West calls this the rule of "Play Happy or Don't Play," and it's a fine piece of advice. A negative attitude will distract you, throw off your play, and destroy your chances of winning.

For this reason, don't attach unnecessary stress or negative emotions to your poker game. If you're at the card club to win cash for the bills, you should *not* be there. Nor should you be playing if you are dead set on getting "revenge" for the rough session you had the last time you played, nor if you're ticked off because your card buddy teased you for playing poorly at your last game. While you, of course, want to come out ahead any time you play, you must realize that not everyday can you be a winner. Sometimes, the cards just might not fall. Maybe you'll stay in, only to see your 10s full of deuces (10 10 10 2 2) lose to queens full of 8s (Q Q Q 8 8). Sometimes these things happen.

When you play poker, you should always remain calm. Be in a good mood before heading down to play. If you're angry, or feeling pressure to earn money you badly need, stay away from the poker table. Work off your anger at the gym or pick up some overtime hours. When you are playing, it's also crucial to watch yourself and avoid hasty bets or foolish raises. Don't let boredom destroy your careful, strategic play.

When you've been sitting there for an hour and not had a chance to play many hands, it can be all too tempting to chase cards. You start to think, "Well, I've got an ace and a king," ignoring someone else's ace and king staring at you from the board. Maybe you decide to throw in a buck to see more cards. Pretty soon, that short stack that was in front of you is gone, and you're reaching in your wallet for another fifty-dollar bill. Stud is a game of patience. Play a hand only when you think you have something with a good chance of improving.

Going on "Tilt"

"My game was going fine, and then I lost a few close hands and went on tilt." Ever heard such a phrase from a poker player? When a player speaks of going on **tilt**, he's talking about losing his patience and playing recklessly. If you do that, you turn from a card player into a magician who, as his first trick, makes the stack of chips in front of him vanish.

It's easy for anyone to go on tilt. A player on tilt stops using sound judgment, and starts playing anything. Maybe he suffered a bad beat from another player and is now out to "get him" by staying in with hands he shouldn't be playing. A player on tilt is desperately hoping that the trash hand he's holding will transform itself into something good if he stays in to see all seven cards. Nine times out of ten, that trash hand will go from a little bit of trash to a lot of trash, and the player will lose a lot of money in the process. If you feel yourself getting too frustrated, pick up your chips and cash them in. Go for a walk until you feel you are levelheaded enough to play well again.

Don't Be Intimidated!

Along with maintaining a positive attitude, it's also important not to be intimidated when you play in a public card room. If you're new to the game, it's natural to feel that you're in the presence of "pros," but at the low limits, you aren't likely to find too many professionals (though at times you will find plenty of people who *think* they are).

Relax and have a good time. If you have a general knowledge of the game, but you're still vague about certain concepts, don't hesitate to ask questions. Most dealers are competent and friendly, and they'll be glad to help you.

Don't worry about looking foolish or making a mistake; there will be occasions when you bet the wrong amount or misread a hand. You won't get thrown out of the card room. As the saying goes, "You can't learn to swim if you don't jump in the water." You may very well be nervous the first sessions you have in a public card room, but think of each session as a chance to improve your game and implement your strategies. As time goes on, your play will improve. Let's take a look at some easy ways you can quickly become a better player.

Remembering Cards

Some people like Texas hold 'em because there are no cards to remember – you have your hole cards in front of you, and the rest of the cards are always on the board. In stud, there's more work to do, which brings us to the concept of live cards.

There is a saying that Texas hold 'em is a game of big cards, while stud is a game of live cards. That's very true. After you're dealt your first three cards, if you are considering staying in or are the forced bring-in bet, the very first thing you must do is look at the board to see what's out there. As players muck their cards, you need to keep in mind what they've folded. If you find it too tough to remember everything that was folded, at the very least you must be on the lookout at all times for cards that would have helped your hand that are gone. For example, let's say you have two kings in the hole and an 8 upcard. A hidden big pair – very nice. But it's worthless if the other two kings have been dealt.

Remembering cards is one of the most difficult aspects of the game, and I continue to work on it. I seem to have no problem remembering *my* cards, but it gets trickier when I try to remember all the cards that have passed. A basic thing you can do is pay sharp attention at all times to the cards as they are folded, and at the end of each betting round, put them in some type of order mentally (such as from smallest to largest or vice-versa). Obviously, there's no need to memorize the cards on the board – they're right in front of you.

In case you're not yet convinced of the value of remembering cards, I'll give you an example. One session, I played in a game where I had filled up on fifth street: 4s full of kings. I played this aggressively, but several players stayed in to the river, including one player who had two pair on the board, 3s and 9s.

Because I had been paying attention, I remembered that one of his 9s was gone – there was only one card left in the deck that could help him beat me. As it turned out, he had 3s full of 9s, and I managed to win a nice pot. Remembering cards may not be the easiest thing in the world to do, but if you want to play stud well, there's simply no way around it.

THE GAME OF 7-CARD STUD

Check Out Other Games

Before you take a seat, it's a good idea to take a look at the games that are underway. If you can, request to be at a particular game. Take a look and see how the games are going – whether there seem to be a lot of people calling anything, or if one player is constantly raising.

During the course of a game, if you feel frustrated by the way it's going, you can always call a floor person and ask to be moved to an available seat in another game. Some games will have players who are more conservative (tighter), and some games will have players who throw a lot of money at many pots (looser). I've found that games at the card club on weekday mornings and afternoons are more tight, as there are many retirees there who play more conservatively. On evenings and weekends, you have a more diverse crowd. Many people are there to just have a good time, and as a result, they play more loosely.

The Importance of Odds

Any gambler knows the importance of statistical odds, which play a huge role in poker. If you don't take the time to learn them, you will be at a major disadvantage. In the back of this book, in the Appendix, I've listed the odds for different types of hands. As in any poker game, there are two types of odds – pot odds and the odds for making your hand, statistical odds.

Pot odds are not that difficult. If you know how much is in the pot, you can figure out the pot odds by dividing that sum by your bet. If there is $40 in the pot, for example, and it is a $4 bet to you, your pot odds are 10 to 1. If these are greater than the statistical odds of making that hand, then it's a good bet. Let's say you started out with three to a flush, which didn't improve on fourth street. At this point, your statistical odds of making your flush are 8.5 to 1. But, if there's a lot of money in the pot and you're getting large enough pot odds, it is okay to toss in another bet.

Knowing statistical odds is essential, so memorize the odds that are listed in the back of the book. It's always helpful to know pot odds and compare the two, but at the very least have a general idea of the drawing odds so you know how likely you are to make the hand you want to make. If you can do both, great. With so much betting going on, you might find it very hard to count the chips which are in a big pile in the center of the table while simultaneously trying to pay attention to what has been folded. If that's the case, focus on the cards first.

Knowing odds will help you at the table, but remembering those cards is more important. The odds give you a general idea of your chances of success, but if you do not know which of the cards that you need are live and which ones are dead, then the odds are useless. In the earlier example, while I may be an 8.5 to 1 shot to get my flush on fourth street, I am much more likely to call if I know that very few cards of my needed suit had been dealt to other players.

THE GAME OF 7-CARD STUD

Study Your Opponents

Another important aspect of stud poker (and any poker game) is to know your opponents. You must always be paying attention to the players at the table and watching their style of play. Are they the kind of players who seem to be calling every single time someone bets? If so, you can take advantage of them when you have the monster hand, because you know they will go ahead and call. Are they the type of players who seem to fold constantly and bet hard when they do stay in? (Ideally, you are this type of player – it's known as "tight-aggressive," and we'll get to that shortly.)

Maybe your opponents are the type of players who seem to bet with anything. Knowing your opponents' style is very important. It will help you to get insight into how they play – whether they are playing smart or just chasing cards.

While you will be playing only a few hands, that doesn't mean that you shouldn't be watching your opponents like a hawk and getting information on them at all times. At my card club, there are lots of televisions everywhere, and people are naturally interested in the horse races or highlights on *Sportscenter*. You can watch TV at home. If you've made the effort to come to the card room to play cards, your focus should be on the game, not on the TV.

Even when you fold, watch the action – work on remembering cards or on watching what your opponents stay in with. Look at their eyes; notice how they breathe when the cards are dealt to them. Does one player sit and stare at a hand at length before betting? If so, odds are he doesn't have that great of a hand – if he did, he'd be betting it. Does one player seem to be staring at the ball game constantly? If that's the case, you want to take advantage of him, because the poker game is of secondary importance to him.

Another way to get a good idea of how your opponents play is by noticing what their hole cards are when they lay down their hands. When the last card is dealt, if that card goes on top, the two starting cards are on the bottom; if it goes on the bottom, the two starting hole cards are on the top. A player will sometimes shuffle the three hidden cards, but it's not too tough to figure out what he started with. If he rose on third street and then turns over two kings and a 5, he likely had two kings from the beginning.

Betting Styles
Just as in life there are many different personalities, at the poker table there are many different types of bettors. Sometimes you'll see a player who likes to bang away and seems to be staying in every type of hand. Other times it might seem like a player isn't even in the game because he never bets. So, what are the differences? And who's in between those extremes?

Loose-Passive
One common type of player that you will see at the low limits is called the **loose-passive** type. To this player's

thinking, poker is a way to pass a few hours – and hopefully come out ahead. The only way he can come out ahead, he tells himself, is to see all the cards. Only if he has absolute trash will he fold – and sometimes even then he won't. Because he's also passive, though, he isn't likely to bang away very much, even when he should be doing so. Unless he has an absolute monster hand, he'll just casually call everything in sight in the hope that he gets something good and wins the pot.

Sometimes these players will walk away from a session a winner, but more often than not, they'll just be giving their money away to other players, including you. Many players of low-limit stud fall into this category. When you think you're playing at a table that is loose-passive, dollar signs should flash before your eyes, because when you get that monster hand, it will pay off nicely.

The Maniac

Along with the loose-passive type of player, from time to time you will run into what is known as "the maniac." This kind of player can be called **loose-aggressive.** Many people enjoy playing with one of these, because they know the player isn't thinking clearly and is there just to get a rush from betting high amounts (and from winning a huge pot if he does win one). This player may have an ace-high on his third card and be raising. He likes to bluff a lot, too, so he may think that he can raise all he wants and drive out all the other players. This player will always lose money in the long run.

Personally, while I can win some good money with someone like this at the table, and take advantage of him when I have something, I prefer not to play with a maniac. Against a maniac, I risk losing a lot of money on one hand that would have cost me less to play had I been with the loose-passive players. Again, there is nothing wrong with playing with this kind of player. Just realize that during that session, you may see a lot of fluctuations in the number of chips in front of you.

The Rock

Another kind of player you'll see at the card room is the **tight-passive** type, also known as "the rock." This type of player knows exactly what kinds of hands he wants to bet, and he stays far away from anything that is risky. This kind of player plays very smartly – he never chases cards that he shouldn't. You will not be making much money from this type of player. At the same time, the tight-passive style of player won't make much money for himself, either. While these players may know precisely what they should and should not play with, they do not bet properly. For instance, rather than raise when they have good hands, they will just call.

Unlike in hold 'em, in stud, even when you have a great hand, there is always the chance – no matter how small – that you will lose to a bigger hand. This fear is always in the back of the rock's mind. He just wants to win the pot, even if it is small, and he does not want to put a lot of his own chips at stake in the process. While this may seem to save him money, in reality he does not win nearly as much as he should over the long run. By just calling bets and not betting aggressively, he's allowing the weaker hands to stay in cheaply, and many times that one weak hand will improve just enough – often on the last card – to beat what should have been the best hand – his hand.

Who You Want To Be

There's a saying in the movie *Ocean's Eleven* that goes something like this: the only way to beat the house is when you bet, to bet really big. Now, of course, there's no house to beat in poker, but the saying can be applied to the table to describe the type of player that you want to be: **tight-aggressive.**

As this type of player, you are not going to play many hands. Nine times out of ten, your first three cards will be in the muck. When you do play, though, you play properly. You know when it's best to call to build the pot odds in your favor. You also know when it's right to raise either to force other players out of the hand or to make them pay if they are trying to draw to larger hands. Playing this style will help you to maximize the amount of chips that are in your pile by not wasting them on lousy hands but taking more from your opponents when the big hand that you want finally hits.

We've now covered the basics of what you need to know before taking a seat at the card table. We've also looked at the different styles of players that you might encounter out there. Before we go into the proper ways to play at each stage in stud poker, let's take a moment to discuss bluffing.

The Bluff

Most people are familiar with the concept of bluffing – trying to represent a big hand when you have nothing. There's even a variation of the "dogs playing poker" art series called "A Bold Bluff," in which one dog has a huge stack of chips he bet in front of him on a pair of deuces. Movies are also full of great poker scenes in which a player tries to bluff his way into winning a big pot.

Naturally, since I love poker and love to outplay my opponent, winning a large pot when I had nothing would give me a lot of satisfaction. I, however, rarely bluff.

Proceed with Caution

Loving poker like I do, you may say to yourself, "But isn't bluffing a part of the game?" It certainly is. Maybe you've watched the World Series of Poker, and you've seen a player pull off a successful bluff. You've certainly seen it in the movies. So, why shouldn't you bluff all that much? The answer is that this isn't the movies, and it certainly isn't the World Series of Poker.

At the low limits, bluffing rarely works. You will frequently find the game to be full of many loose-passive players, also known as "calling stations." Whether you have nothing or a good hand, at least one player is likely to call you. Does this mean you can never bluff? No, but if you do, you should put a lot of consideration into it before you do so (which will not be that often).

THE GAME OF 7-CARD STUD

If You're Considering a Bluff...

First, if you are going to try to pull off a bluff, you need to have been at the table at least an hour. This will have given you a chance to know your opponents a little better. After an hour, you will have watched how they play and gotten a feel for which types of players they are. Will they stay in with anything? Or are they low-action "rocks" who stay in only when they have something? More often than not, your opponents will be a mixture of the two types of players.

Second, if you decide to try a bluff, it's important that you have remembered cards. For instance, say you are on sixth street, and the card that falls gives you four to a flush showing on the board. This is a scary hand, but if you've remembered your cards, you can bet casually. Again, re-membering the cards is important. If you've counted a lot of your suit on the board, don't consider bluffing. Many of the players at your table will not have any clue how many of your suit are live or dead, but there will be a few good players who *have* been paying attention.

A player who has seen many of your needed cards fall will have no problem calling your bluff. With few of your suit on the board, by betting here on sixth street, you may pull off a "semi-bluff" – you may be able to represent a hand that you don't currently have, but could get on the seventh card (also known as **the river**). The same circum-stances apply when you have four to a straight showing or two pair showing – you may not have your hand, but you could complete it on the river.

When you do get to the last card, if you don't complete your hand, you can try for the bluff again – if there are remaining players and you know their styles. For example, let's say you have two pair on the board, and it's checked to you after you get your seventh card. Wanting to bluff, your first instinct might be not even to look at that seventh card, just to toss four chips in front of you.

This may sound like a good idea – you'd like to send the message that you completed your hand by sixth street, so you have no need even to look at the seventh card. Do *not* do this. Always look at that last card. Your doing so keeps your opponents confused – now they don't know if you had your hand on sixth street or just got it on the river.

Hopefully you did get your card, and you won't even have to bluff. If you did not, and you want to bluff in this situation, you should have a four-flush, four-to-a-straight or two pair on the board. You also should not have seen many other of your needed cards fall during the play of the hand. Look at your seventh card before betting. Try to remain as calm as possible – don't shake your hands, sigh or make a lot of eye movements, and casually bet your chips if you feel you must bluff. Don't stare at your hand long. Look quickly at what you're holding, then look at your chips, and bet if you feel bluffing is the best move.

Here's another reason bluffing can be beneficial – even if you do not pull it off, it can confuse your opponents. Suppose you have just a four-flush, and, because you've not seen many of your suit fall during the course of play, you bet on the river. One player calls you with his two-pair, and he's overjoyed to see you don't have that fifth heart. Now, down the road, when you do have a big hand, you may get more people calling your river bet to "keep you honest." Then you will joyfully turn over your flush that you did make.

Why You Shouldn't Bluff

Even looking at the situations when you *can* bluff, it is still best *not* try to pull off a bluff. Again, we're not playing $30/$60 stud, in which the players are very good and they play a solid, tight-aggressive game. Bluffing is more likely to occur in that game. At low limits, a lot of people will stay in to see the last card. With four players having stayed to the end, and with a decent sized pot, more often than not, bluffing simply will not work, because at least one player will be determined to "keep you honest."

Nonetheless, as I've already said, an occasional bluff can work out in one of two ways:

1. You will win some money by getting players to fold then and there.
2. You will increase the size of a pot down the road by getting players to stay with you because they saw you bluff earlier on.

Despite those benefits, I cannot emphasize enough that you must keep in mind that bluffing should not be foremost on your mind when you take a seat at a low-limit stud game. You should bluff very rarely, and only when you have gotten a feel for your opponents and have been paying sharp attention to the cards.

The Buy-In

One last topic before we move on: the buy-in. How much in chips should you bring to the table? A good rule-of-thumb is to start with ten times the high-end of the table limit. I primarily play at $2-$4 limit, so I will generally start with at least $40.

Here's one more thing to consider: unless you came not planning to spend more than $40, make sure that you always have enough in front of you to call or raise should you get a good hand. For example, if you are down to $4, and you get a good hand, about all you can do is go "all-in," which will result in the creation of another pot in which you will have no stake. Always buy at least another $20 in chips when you're running below $10. You want to have enough chips in front of you to call or bang away with a good hand so you can win all of a big pot and not just a smaller main pot.

3

THIRD STREET

From this point on, our focus will be on how to play each hand and what you need to keep in mind as you play. I will always emphasize "tight-aggressive" play. While my strategies can apply to any low-limit game, the examples I'll give are from a game that has a $2/4 betting structure.

Trips

Every once in a great while the poker gods will bless you with three-of-a-kind on your first three cards. Don't plan on seeing this very often – it's happened to me only a few times, and I've played a lot of hands. When it does happen to you, though, know how to play the hand properly.

Many players think that this hand is a good one to play slowly. They believe there's no possible way they can lose with it, and that they will inevitably improve later. They just play slowly to deceive other players and give themselves time to visualize how big the pot that they're going to win will become.

Playing this hand slowly isn't always the best course of action. If you have three jacks or better, it's fine just to call before you pick up the action and bet more strongly later on. If you have smaller sets of trips, though, you want to raise as much as possible right away. Why? Because you become very vulnerable to being outdrawn.

Suppose you have three 4s. An opponent with a pair of 5s limps in for a buck, and on fourth street he catches a third 5. Now, suddenly, what started out looking wonderful is terrible. Instead of being the favorite, you are an underdog.

When you start out with a smaller set of trips, *always* raise – it's better to win a small pot than to lose a lot of money trying to win a large one. Smaller sets of trips are more vulnerable – when you're holding them, one of your opponents is all too likely to complete a larger three-of-a-kind in the course of play. Try to force your opponents out before that happens.

Quick Guide...
...to *Trips* on *Third Street:*
• **RAISE** if you think a lot of people will stay in, or if your trips are smaller (such as trip deuces). Always re-raise if someone has already raised the betting. Bring it in for the full amount if you are first to act.
• **CALL** if you have a big set of trips (10s or better). Don't bang away until the later rounds.

Big Pairs

While it's rare to be dealt rolled up trips, you will often find yourself with a good pair (10s or better) at the start. A good pair is always a great starting hand, particularly if your pair is hidden, because that prevents your opponents from knowing the real strength of your hand right away. A hidden pair can also help you as the betting rounds progress.

When I first started playing, I automatically assumed that when I had a good pair on third street, raising was the right move. If it was a dollar to me, I'd make it two without a second thought; if two to me, I'd make it four. Many times this is exactly the right move, but not always. Let's take a moment to look at some examples.

Banging Away vs. Proceeding Cautiously

When should you bang away and when should you play more cautiously? When you have been dealt a pair of 10s or better, the first thing you must do, as with any hand, is look out across the board to see what else is out there. Your big pair may look great, but it's worthless if the other two cards you need have already been dealt. If one of your cards has been dealt, you'll want to limp in if your pair is split and raise if your pair is in the hole. You can raise with a split pair at times, even if a card you need to improve is gone, but you must have a good kicker.

For example, suppose you have a pair of 10s in the hole and an ace on the board. You see another ten but no other aces. In this case, raise – make those drawing and marginal hands think twice about sticking around. You have a great kicker here so you can be a bit more loose. Most of your opponents will probably figure you for a pair of aces.

If all your cards are live, that's great. It's often the case that the decision to raise or limp in will come down to live cards. If you had the same pair of 10s and ace kicker and both another ten *and* another ace were on the board, you should just limp in, not raise. This situation shows the importance of live cards and the need to be aware of which cards are live and which ones are not.

Another thing to do when you're deciding whether to raise or just limp in with your big pair is to look to your left to see who has yet to bet. You may be feeling great about your pocket 10s, but before you raise, check to see what the other players have who have yet to bet. If you see two or more cards that are bigger than yours, just limp in. If it is raised from the bring-in of a dollar to two dollars, go ahead and call. If it's re-raised, think carefully about calling. The only time you should call a re-raise in this situation is when you have a large kicker and all of your cards are live.

The Importance of Position
Position can never be underestimated. The later you are to act, the better. For example, suppose you are holding J J 4 and you're the second-to-last player to bet. The low card brought in the betting for a dollar, the next three players called, and the next two folded. You look to your left and see a 10, and out on the board among those who have bet

are two queens and a king.

Earlier on, I stated that if these players had not yet bet, limping in was the proper move. Here, you can go ahead and complete the bring-in to two dollars. The 10 to your left will probably fold, and because there was no raising by the larger cards on the board, it's likely those players do not have split pairs.

Your raise will get at least one or two of the remaining players out, which is what you want to happen. Against any drawing hand heads up, you'll be a favorite with a big pair. If there are a lot of hands in the pot, though, you've gone from a favorite to an underdog. Odds are, with all players sticking around (and they will if you do not make them pay) you will get outdrawn by somebody.

While later position is usually best, at times early position can be advantageous. When you're in early position, you won't know what the players to your left will do. If, however, you have a big pair that is higher than pairs that could be represented by the rest of the board, you should raise. By raising the bring in from a dollar to two dollars, you'll probably cause more players behind you to fold.

One thing that I have found playing the lower limits is that while late position is ideal, if I raise with a strong pair in early position, more of the players yet to act will fold than if I raised in late position with the same hand. Why? Because at the lower limits, people's thinking goes, "I've already got a buck in the pot, and it's only one more chip to see another card." Players foolishly put another chip in even after having been raised, because they don't want you to "steal" their money.

Even though most of the players might stay in with a late position raise because they have some money in the pot, you still should never, ever let them get away with sticking around cheaply with a drawing hand. Yes, many may stay in, but if even one or two drop, it's of benefit to you. You are cutting the field, and with a starting big pair, that's exactly what you want to do.

> ## Quick Guide...
> ### ...to *Big Pairs* on *Third Street*
> • **RAISE** most (about 99%) of the time, unless you find a reason not to play them fast (e.g. if both of your other cards for trips are dead).
> • **CALL** only if your game is so loose that you know without a doubt that other players will stay in despite your raise.

Middle Pairs

Many players make the mistake of raising with *any* pair. They believe that a pair, even if it's just a middle one, is some type of monster hand on third street. The automatic thing to do? Toss out another chip or two to raise the bet. More often than not, this habit will cost you money in the long run, unless your cards are all live and you have an excellent kicker.

THIRD STREET

Kickers - The Bigger, The Better

There's that word again: *kicker*. I touched on it in the previous chapter, when I noted that a big pair is great, but it's even better with a big kicker to boot. With a medium pair, a big kicker is even more important, whether your pair is hidden or split. Why? The answer should become clear if you just take a moment to think about it. Let's say you have a pair of pocket 7s, with a king on the board, and you're in middle position. Looking around the board, you see no other 7s or kings. Cool.

The action comes to you, and, when you see nothing too threatening to your left, you raise. Ideally, you are hoping to make trips by fifth street in this situation, but by having a good kicker, you have another way to get a solid two pair. Additionally, when you have a high kicker showing on the board in this situation, it can be especially beneficial when you pair the door card, because by having raised on third street, you will cause many players to figure you for trip kings on fourth street.

Now that we've looked at this situation in which you have a pair, a good kicker, and all of your cards to improve your pair live, you should realize that you should raise in this situation if there aren't too many scary cards out there left to bet. Just call if you're in a game where there is a lot of third street raising or if there are more than two visible bigger cards yet to bet.

Be Careful with Lousy Kickers

Here's a different situation. You are holding a split pair of

41

6s with a 3 (or "trey") as your kicker. Not cool. Sure, you have a pair, but you can't be too happy about it. In this situation, if you decide to play at all, you will want just to limp in. With a lousy kicker, you can get into a *lot* of trouble down the road if you stay in too long. You'll have 6s and treys, and nine times out of ten, unless you fill up, this hand won't be winning you very much money. So, with a middle pair and a lousy kicker, just limp in.

In my experience at the low limits, there often isn't much raising going on at third street, so it's worth a chip to see fourth. But, *all* of your 6s in this situation must be live. If there's just one other 6 out there, muck your cards. It isn't worth even a buck to see another card when only one card in the deck can improve a pair (which had a mediocre kicker and wasn't even all that good to begin with.)

Note that while in most low-limit games there's not a lot of raising going on in third street play, this is not true of *all* games. I've played in games where people aren't afraid to cap the betting at third street if they feel they have a good enough hand. With a medium pair, even if you have a good kicker, if it is more than two bets back to you (e.g. you put in a dollar, it was raised to two, then to four, making it three dollars to call), definitely fold. Yes, you spent a dollar. Do you really want to spend three more in this situation to go in as a probable underdog to a big pair or, worse yet, to rolled up trips? I don't think so.

Two final points that I've tried to hammer home throughout the book thus far: remember the cards and always keep in mind your position. If, while you're watching the race at Belmont on the TV monitor, you suddenly hear the dealer say, "The bet's to you, Sir," and you look down to see a split medium pair but have missed the two other guys who have folded, I hope you'd just fold. In this situation, you have no clue what cards have been mucked.

Before you go banging away with a medium pair, check to see who has yet to act. If you see some big cards out there, limp in with your live pair that has a good kicker, and muck it if your kicker is lousy. One thing I've certainly learned is that medium pairs are nothing but trouble if you have a dead card on the board or a lousy kicker with big cards in your opponents' hands. Save yourself the anxiety and the chips and wait for a better hand.

Quick Guide...
...to *Middle Pairs* on *Third Street*

• **RAISE** if you have an excellent kicker and *all* live cards, and if you're confident doing so will drive out other players.

• **CALL** most of the time – particularly if your kicker is high.

• **FOLD** if there is heavy action before it gets to you, or if you have a lousy kicker and one of your cards to improve to trips is dead.

Low Pairs

Play of small pairs (deuces through 5s) will be much the same as play of middle pairs. The biggest difference that arises concerns the kicker, which is essential to consider if you're thinking of playing small pairs. When playing them, it is very important that either you have a big kicker or that *all* of your cards needed to improve to trips are live. Ideally, both of these will be the case. If you have a dead kicker, you can limp in with your low pair anyway, but *all* of your needed cards for trips *must* be live.

It doesn't take a professional to see what will happen if your kicker is low. The odds favor your improving to two pair before improving to trips, so having a lousy kicker can just get you into trouble should you improve to two pair. That said, can a medium or low two pair ever be played? Yes, in certain situations, which we'll cover at fourth street.

Having your pair hidden is always better than having a split pair, but that's especially true with small pairs. As with middle pairs, if you should pair your visible big kicker, many players will believe you have trips. For example, suppose you are in middle position and have a pair of treys in the hole with a king on the board. You limp in for a dollar, and you pick up another king. This gives you a great two pair, and many of your opponents will fear that you have trips. As a result, you can force them out by playing that two pair hard.

THIRD STREET

When to Fold

Many players are tempted to play any pair – even a split pair of deuces with a 4 for a kicker and a dead deuce. They have that mindset that any pair is better than nothing, and it's hard to shake. It's especially tempting to play any pair when you've been dealt absolutely nothing for an hour. In fact, during one session in which I had gone a long time without playing a hand, I once caught myself *raising* with a split pair of 6s and a 9 kicker!

Can a low pair with a mediocre kicker be played at all? Yes, it can, but you must be certain of two things. One is that there is next to *zero* chance you will be raised (and that's highly unlikely). Ideally, you will be in late position, so you'll already know what the other players have done. Second, you'll want all of your needed cards for trips to be live unless your kicker is excellent – if even one is gone, then, unless you were the bring-in, you should be gone, too.

> ## Quick Guide...
> ### ...to *Low Pairs* on *Third Street:*
> • **CALL** if you have a good kicker and live cards, and you're confident that the pot will not be raised. With low pairs, you want to stay in for as few chips as possible.
> • **FOLD** if someone has completed the betting, unless you know that player to be very loose – no need to start out from behind. You also need to fold if one of your cards to improve to trips is dead or if you have a lousy kicker.

Flush Draws

When I started playing stud, it was easy to get caught up in my own little world. I would get dealt three suited cards and automatically be reaching for my chip pile, ready to throw out a dollar because surely the odds favor my getting my flush by the river, right?

Well, not exactly. So many players fall into the trap of believing that any three suited cards mean great odds for becoming five suited cards. Actually, with three suited cards, odds are still *against* your making your flush. So before you get the vision in your head of the dealer pushing a large pile of chips your way as you lay down your flush, take a few things into consideration.

Quality is Crucial

First, ask yourself about the quality of your hand. Yes, you may have three-to-a-flush, but are your cards a deuce, a 5 and a 7? If that's the case, your hand is not so exciting. When we looked at pairs, we discussed the importance of a good kicker. You cannot have tunnel vision and focus in just on making the flush – you must consider other possibilities for improvement as well.

Your best situation would be to have a jack, queen and king of the same suit, since that hand gives you a lot of ways to improve. You may be thinking "straight flush," here, but that isn't very likely. In fact, it's so unlikely that the card room I go to gives out a free hat if you are fortunate enough to get one. What's more likely to happen with a jack, queen, and king of the same suit is that you'll improve to a straight, a regular flush, or a solid two pair. Remember, with a three-flush, *the bigger your cards are the better*. Of course, you are hoping to improve to a flush, but big cards give you other ways of improving your hand that might make it playable down the line even if you see other cards needed to improve your flush fall elsewhere.

Live Card Requirements

Second, as soon as you get your cards and see that you have three-to-a-flush, start looking around the board. Count how many of your needed cards have been dealt as door cards to other players. If you have three non-face cards and you see two of your needed suit gone, fold. If you have two cards that are 10 or higher, and only three (or fewer) cards of your needed suit are gone, you can stay in for a dollar to see a fourth card.

With any more than three of your needed cards gone, fold. With three-to-a-flush, those three cards you hold may look pretty, but think about it. Even if you have big cards, if four of your needed suit have been dealt, that leaves just six left in the deck (assuming they haven't been dealt to other players). Of those six cards, you need two to make your flush. You may have a few big cards, but it's not worth even another dollar to stay in and hope you'll complete your flush.

The only time you can consider staying in for a dollar to see fourth street is if you have three suited cards in sequence. In this situation, you have another out – drawing to a straight. But, even here, when you're thinking of staying in, make sure that you've looked at the board and counted both how many cards in your needed suit have been dealt, *and* how many cards that would improve your three-straight are out there. If more than two are dead, fold.

Never Raise!

When you do stay in with three suited cards, never raise. It's still a drawing hand, and you want as many people in the pot as possible to increase the pot odds in your favor. Since the statistical odds are against your completing a flush, the more people there are in the pot to start out with the better, because you'll be getting more value on your bet if you complete your hand as play progresses. Raising would drive people out. You want to do that with a big pair, because someone might outdraw you, but here, just call to keep in as many players as you can.

Quick Guide...
...to *Flush Draws* on *Third Street*:
• **CALL** if you see that two or fewer cards of your suit have been dealt. It's okay to stay in with three if you have big cards, and you can stay in with up to four if you have three-to-a-straight-flush.

• **FOLD** if more than two of your suited cards are gone and you have small cards. If you can't resist gambling, *certainly* don't play if it costs more than the bring-in to stay in. With bigger cards, you can stay in with up to three dead cards of your suit.

Straight Draws

Having three cards to a straight on third street is often just as tempting as having three to a flush, and just as many players will play any three suited cards, many players will also play any three cards in a sequence. I must admit, I, too, used to stay in anytime I started out with three to a straight. As I gained experience, though, I came to dislike straight draws. There are even some players who will rarely play those hands. Nonetheless, three-to-a-straight hands are quite playable, but they cannot be played as liberally as flush draws. Different situations will arise in which straight draws can or cannot be played, and we'll cover them now.

Big Cards Are a Must

As with flush draws, a key thing to remember with your straight draws is that bigger is always better. If you have a ten, a jack, and a queen, you have a very good straight draw. As with the flush, the odds are still against your completing your straight, but with three big cards, more options may present themselves if you're fortunate enough to get a big pair or better down the line.

With three small cards, such as a 4, a 5 and a 6, you can't get too excited. Because all three of your cards are small, completing your straight is about the only thing that will help you. Pairs and even two pairs are pretty much worthless at those ranks.

As with any hand, as soon as you've looked at what you hold, you will want to keep your eyes on the board. When you're on a flush draw with small cards, it is fine to stay when two of your needed suit are on the board, and if you have big cards, up to three of your needed suit can be there. With a straight draw, though, even with three big cards, if you find that more than two of the cards that will improve your three-straight to a four-straight are dead, fold and be done with it.

When you're checking the board to see how many of your cards are dead, the first thing to look for are dead cards that would have improved your three-straight to a four-straight open-ended draw. For example, if you have a 9, a 10, and a jack, the first cards you will be looking for are the 8 and the queen. What about the 7 and the king? You'll need those cards, too, so keep your eye open for any of them. Of primary importance, though, are the cards that create your open-ended straight draws. Remember, if you see two that are gone, you should be gone, too.

Obviously, you can't forget the cards that would complete your straight. If, for instance, you have the above hand, and you see a queen gone along with a king and a 7, fold unless you improve to a pair. While only one of the eight cards that would make your three-straight a four-straight draw is dead, two of the other cards that would complete your straight are gone, too. No need to go against the odds to try to get lucky – wait for something better.

The Essentials
Straight-draws can be very confusing. So, before we move on, let's take another moment to consider what you should

do depending on the situation you face.

First, consider the quality of your hand. If it is a small straight draw, such as a 3, a 4, and a 5, consider folding immediately, even if most of your cards are live. This is a mediocre hand. Even if it turns into a straight, it may very well lose to a better hand. Second, if you decide to play a straight draw, remember, the bigger the better. Third, always be looking at the board. If you see that more than two of the cards to improve to a four-straight are gone, fold. If one card and two secondary cards to make your straight are gone, fold as well.

Never hesitate to fold the small straight-draws, even if you find that all of your needed cards are live. As I have said again and again with flush and straight draws, the bigger the better. When you're drawing to a straight, big cards are especially important.

Stay Away from Gaps

Finally, you may be tempted from time to time to play hands that have a gap between two cards, such as an 8, a 10, and a jack. This is a mistake that *will* cost you money. Three cards to a straight that have a gap in them have a *very small* chance of improving. The only possible situation in which playing this hand is justifiable is if all of your gap cards are live, you are the bring-in, last, or second-to last to act, *and* you have very good cards, such as a jack, a king, and an ace.

The odds are already against your making a straight

with three cards in a sequence. Playing them, especially if they're three small cards in a sequence, can get you in trouble. Playing one-gap straights can get you in even more trouble. If you do feel the urge to play a one-gap straight, make sure all of your gap cards are live, and don't play it unless you are one of the last players to act and have three big cards.

> ## Quick Guide...
> ### ...to *Straight Draws* on *Third Street:*
> • **CALL** an open-ended straight if two or fewer of your cards are dead and no other player has raised. Calling a full small bet is okay if *all* of your cards are live, but don't call more than that.
> • **FOLD** if there is a lot of action or if more than two of your cards to an open-ended straight are dead.

The Best of the Rest

We have now looked at just about every hand that you can start with on third street – the pairs and the drawing hands. In nearly every other situation, you will have folded if you don't have a pair or drawing hand to start out with, and you'll be paying attention to how the play of the hand progresses. There are just a few other situations in which you can limp in to see fourth street.

One is, of course, when you are the bring-in and no one has raised. Here, you'll be staying in with anything. You can also limp in for a dollar if you are in late position, have three big cards, see that most of them are live and have had few callers. For example, suppose you hold a 10, a king, and an ace. You are the last to act, and when you studied the board, you saw a 10 fall, but no kings or aces. By the time it gets to you, there are two people who have stayed in: the original bring-in bet, and one other caller. In this case, go ahead and toss in a chip to see fourth street. Hope that you will improve to a big pair.

Proceed with caution, though. If there are more than three players who have stayed in by the time it gets to you, (or two if you are the second-to-last player to bet and there is a scary card to your left) fold. Yes, you have three big cards, but even a small pair is starting out with something better than you have.

If you hold two suited cards, are in early or middle position, and if all cards that are smaller than any of the cards that you hold have yet to act, you can limp in for a dollar if you feel the need. Still, most of the time, even with three big cards and smaller cards yet to act, save yourself the dollar – wait for the better starting hand. Of course, it's tempting to play – you've taken the time to come down to the card club, and you want to be in the hand. But if your objective is to maximize your winnings, select your three cards very, very carefully.

Remember – the decision you make on third street will be your most important decision on a hand. The gambler inside you may urge you to play more loosely, but that's a foolish mistake that's all too easy to make. Trash is more likely just to become more trash. Be patient and wait for the hand that you want to play, and when that hand does come, know how to play it properly.

Quick Quiz: Third Street

Before you move on to learn about play on fourth street, take this 10-question quiz to test your knowledge of correct third street play. If you find any questions too difficult, remember that all the information you'll need to answer them is contained in this chapter. Answers are provided directly after the questions.

Questions

1. You hold pocket jacks with a deuce on the board and are the bring-in bet. Do you bring it in for a dollar or the full amount?

2. You have pocket jacks and a 5 on the board and are in late position. The bring-in brought it in for a dollar, there were five callers, and it's to you. Do you call or complete the betting to two dollars?

3. You have rolled up treys and are in middle position. A player holding a queen raises the bring-in bet to two dollars, and it's to you. Do you call or raise?

4. You have the 10 of diamonds, 8 of diamonds, and 5 of diamonds, and you see two other diamonds on the board. It's a dollar to call – do you stay in?

5. You have the king of diamonds, the ace of diamonds, and the jack of diamonds, and you see three other diamonds on the board but no kings or aces. It's one dollar to you to stay in – do you?

6. You have three-to-a-straight – a 4, a 5, and a 6, and you are in late position. The bring-in bet is raised by a queen and then re-raised by an ace, making it four dollars by the time it gets to you. All of your 3s and 7s are live. Do you call?

7. You hold a split pair of 5s and a 7 for a kicker, and you're in early position. One 5 is gone, and a queen, a king and an ace are yet to act. It's one dollar to you to call. Do you stay in or fold?

8. You have pocket aces and a jack on the board. One ace is dead, and the bring-in has been completed to two dollars by a queen on the board. Do you call or raise?

9. You have a suited ace and king in the hole, and a 10 of another suit for your door card. The bring-in was completed to two dollars by a jack. Do you stay-in?

10. You have a split pair of 4s with an ace kicker. No other 4s are dead, and you are in middle position. It's a dollar to you, and several face cards are yet to act. Do you fold, call, or raise?

Answers

1. Bet the full amount. You have a good starting hand. You want to force out other drawing hands early on so they won't give you trouble down the line.

2. Complete it. Yes, at the low limits with only a dollar to call many of the players will stay in – they have some money in the pot and don't want to be pushed around.

If you think there is absolutely no chance that anybody will fold, you can simply call. Most of the time, though, you want to complete it in this situation. That warns other players that you have something, and even if you force out just one player, that's one fewer drawing hand that you have to worry about.

3. Raise. Conventional wisdom says to call to keep as many players in as possible whenever you start out with trips. With a lower set (such as treys), though, raise it to four dollars. You'll force some people out. Better to have the competition out of the way now so if the trips don't improve, someone won't outdraw you.

4. Call. Calling is the right decision, but proceed with caution. As play progresses, you want your cards to be as live as possible, because your hand is not that big. With just two of your needed suit gone, calling is the right decision.

5. Call. With three of your needed suit already gone, folding is a good idea, but not here. Here you have big, live cards to go along with your three-flush.

6. Fold. With just one dollar to call, it's fine to call this bet. But with four dollars to call, well, all you have is a lousy small three-straight. You're going up against a probable big pair. It'd be better to be the big pair than you at this point, so fold the hand.

7. Fold. Yes, you have a pair, but it's a small pair with one card already gone. Only one card can improve you to trips, and a two pair here, being so small, is worthless. Calling would just get you into trouble down the line, so wait until you have a better hand.

8. Raise. One of your aces may be dead, but you have a good kicker, your aces are hidden, and you want to force out as many players as possible. Ideally it will be just you and the player who completed the betting for fourth street.

9. Fold. This was a trick question of sorts for hold 'em players. Any hold 'em player knows that holding a suited ace and king in the hole is very valuable. In stud those cards are not nearly as valuable. Here you have three decent cards, but no pair, no three flush, and no three-straight. The betting has already been completed to two dollars. Rather than put two dollars in the pot, wait until you have something better to work with – you don't want to go up against a probable pair of queens from the start.

10. Call. On third street, there won't be too much banging away at low limits, even from face cards. It's only a dollar to you, your cards are live, and you already have a pair with a good kicker to go along with it. You should try to make trips or a good two pair on fourth street, so go ahead and call.

4

FOURTH STREET

Whether to play past third street is the most important decision you'll make in any hand, but almost as important is knowing how to play each stage of the hand. As play progresses, you will need to know how to play your hand properly based on how much it improves or how much potential it has to improve. In this chapter, we'll look at the different scenarios that unfold at fourth street, and I will explain how to play each hand and when you need to get out and wait for the better hand.

Trips

When you have a large set of trips at third street, slow-playing is your best option. You have a great hand, and you want to keep other players in on the action. Ideally, you'll take their money by the time you get to the last card.

You can continue slow-playing on fourth street, but you must do so cautiously. If you decide to slow play your hand by checking or betting the minimum amount, and there is a pair on the board, no more than two cards that would improve your trips can be gone. For example, let's say you start out with rolled up queens, and you're dealt a

9. Looking around, you see no other queens and only one 9. Slow-playing the hand is the right move here. Your trips are hidden, so you should bet the maximum if you can. Since they can't see a pair on the board, players will not figure you for trips.

You could also slow-play that same hand on fourth street if you started out with 9-Q-Q and then picked up the third queen there. Your pair on the board will intimidate people, and if you check it or just bet the minimum, many of your opponents will assume that the pair is all you have. If you play it slowly, you can keep people in until fifth street, when the betting amounts will increase.

While the above two paragraphs may make slow-playing sound like a good idea, different circumstances call for different ways of playing trips on fourth street. What follows are some key points to keep in mind when you're deciding whether to play your trips hard and fast or slowly.

Position

First, consider your position. Remember that the later it is, the better. Consider this example. You have pocket 4s and a 7 for a door card, and the dealer blesses you with a third 4. If you are one of the last players to act, you will get clues as to what the other players have been dealt based on how they bet. For instance, if a player bets two dollars, it could be an indication that he has either made a set of trips as well or has made a strong two pair. Suppose someone else then raised him. Should you raise or call?

If you see a pair on the board larger than your set of trips, proceed with caution, especially if it belongs to the raiser. He could very well have you beat. If the bet and the raise came from players showing no pairs on the board higher than your trips, raise to force either them or other players out. Being in late position, you have the advantage of having seen these bets. With players yet to act, play your hand hard (bet aggressively) if you feel that they are on drawing hands, such as a four-flush or four-straight. Be sure to play hard if your trips are higher than other pairs showing on the board.

The Paired Door Card

During the course of play, you will frequently see players pair their door cards. Again, any time you see pairs on the board *lower* than the trips you have, bang away. Because of the loose nature of most low-limit games, a pair is simply too hard to toss before fifth street, so your bet likely won't force out those people who should have folded their lower pairs.

When a pair on the board is higher than the rank of your trips (meaning that if the player had trips he would have you beaten), you must proceed with caution. Again, this is why it is essential that you have been paying attention to the play of the hand. Ask yourself – did that player raise on third street or just limp in? If he raised, there's a good chance he may have made trips, so you should just call. (You could fold, but it's best to call to see one more card – if he continues to bang away on fifth street and you do not improve, fold there.)

If your opponent with the high pair just limped in, he *could* have two pair. In many cases, though, he'll have just the pair on the board. When a player pairs the door card (especially if it's a pair like 10s or higher), he may bet the maximum. This may seem scary, but in many instances he's trying to buy the pot. This is especially true with aces. Low-limit players love a pair of aces on the board. They frequently believe they can buy a pot with a big bet, since those intimidating aces will scare people off.

You should play cautiously against any big pair on the board, but do not fall into the trap of automatically fearing what may very well be just a pair and nothing more. Only by paying attention to the play of the game and by studying how that particular player has played third street and previous hands will you be able to get a good "feel" for whether he is representing trips or just trying to scare people out so he can win the pot. To reiterate, this is why it is necessary to pay attention to previous hands – so you know what other players stay in with until the end.

Always be more alert when you see a player pair the door card, especially if it could mean he has trips higher than yours. You can muck your hand with a clear conscience if there are two pairs on the board higher than your trips, and one pair has been re-raised by the other. You may very well have those players beaten there, but the odds do not justify sticking around. Remember to play your hand aggressively unless it looks as if you could be beaten already. You have trips, which is a great hand at fourth street. In most cases it will either win you a lot of money or lose you a lot of money. If it doesn't, you probably played the hand incorrectly.

Force Out Those Drawing Hands

Another reason it's often best to raise is that you want to force out the drawing hands. If you are in early or mid-position, you have a chance to make it more difficult for the drawing hands to stick around. If, in those positions, you see several players who have two cards on the board of the same suit or in sequence, bet or raise.

By betting or raising in early and mid-position, it will be easier for you to force them out than it would from late position. Granted, if you were in late position they would have to call your raise, but by raising from early or mid-position, you make them have to call two bets. That's pretty difficult to do unless they have a great chance at making their hands. Those drawing hands may stick around anyway, but if you play aggressively, at the very least one or two will fold. That's good for you when you are up against a drawing hand.

Many players are burned because they let drawing hands stick around when they could have forced them out. The result of this mistake is that the player with the drawing hand turns over a flush at the showdown, saying with a smile, "The river was good to me." Meanwhile, the player who didn't improve his trip jacks on fourth street mucks his hand in disgust. If you play your good cards aggressively, that first player won't stick around to out-draw you. You'll be the one smiling when the dealer pushes the stack of chips your way.

Calling & Folding

When you have trips on fourth street, raising is clearly what you should do most often. There are times, though, when calling or even folding is the right decision. You certainly won't fold with trips very often, but there will be times when that's the right play.

Let's first talk about when to call with trips. Suppose you are in late position with trip 4s. You are waiting for a pair of aces on the board to bet, and before it gets to you, a pair of deuces will have to act as well. The player with the aces brings it in for four dollars, the next several players fold, and the holder of the pair of deuces raises. Now it's eight dollars to you. That's a lot of money for low-limit. Should you re-raise, call or fold?

It's tough, but here you should just call. Raising may understandably be tempting. The deuces raised, which is a good indication that player has made trips. Sure, your trips are higher than his potential trip deuces, but you have to wait for the aces to act again, and that player may very well re-raise.

At this stage, because things have gotten expensive, most of the drawing hands will be gone, and you'll be left with just the two other players. It's one bet back to the pair of aces. If that player re-raises, it's a good indication that he has trip aces. If he just calls, he is likely representing two pair, because with his money in the pot, most players would have a very tough time folding. They'd want to see another card (which is the right thing to do with a solid two pair).

If it's raised and it comes back to you, you can call unless you have seen two of your needed cards to improve to quads or a full house fall. If they did, as tough as it may be, you must fold. Yes, folding with trips is the least desirable of situations. 70% of the time you will be raising with trips. 28% of the time you will be calling. About 2% of the time you will actually have to fold with trips. Those times will be few and far between, and it may take you a lot of courage to throw in your trips, but at times it's worth it.

One of the factors that will play into your decision as to when to fold with trips will be the status of your cards – are they live or dead? If your last card to improve to quads is dead, it's not that big a deal – quads happen rarely. But if two or more of the cards you need to improve your hand to a boat (full house) are gone, either play very aggressively on fourth street (if you're hoping to win the pot right there), or play very cautiously.

Two factors help determine how you will play: the size of your trips and what the board is showing. With no pairs on the board, or with pairs lower than your trips, even if you have two dead cards, you'll want to bang away. Many hands will be won by any set of trips, so when you have them and no one else appears to, you can stay in as long as possible. Make hands that are trying to improve pay.

So when would you fold? The only instance in which to fold is when there are bigger pairs on the board and there has been a lot of action that makes it difficult to call. When none or one of your needed cards to improve is gone, calling to see fifth street is fine.

But if two of your cards are gone, it is two full bets to you, and you can see a bigger pair or two bigger pairs out there, think long and hard about calling. You probably are looking at one or more sets of trips bigger than yours. Is it really worth two full bets to take a chance on the two cards in the deck that can help? Unless the pot is huge and you are getting fantastic pot odds, as tough as it is, fold in this situation.

If you've been paying attention to what is on the board and what has been folded, your play can be much more nuanced. Let's look at an example to illustrate what I mean.

Say you have trip 4s, and it is a four-dollar bet to you. To your left (yet to act) is a pair of jacks. Normally, you would just call the bet and wait to see what that player would do. If you've seen a jack fall, though, go ahead and raise it to eight dollars – make the pair of jacks pay to let you know if he has the last jack in the deck. With that large of a bet and a solid pair on the board, he probably isn't going to re-raise unless he has trips. If you have seen both of a player's needed cards for trips fall, you can bang away no matter what is the rank of his pair.

Quick Guide...

...to *Trips* on *Fourth Street*

• RAISE if:

-It looks like several drawing hands have yet to act

-There are no bigger pairs than yours on the board

-There is a bigger pair yet to act, but you have seen one or two of his needed cards for trips fall.

• **CALL** if it is a full bet back to you and you see a larger pair yet to act. If that player has raised, it is a strong indicator that he has made trips. Think carefully about how to proceed, and consider how many of your kickers are dead.

• **FOLD** if two circumstances combine:

-There is a lot of action from a bigger pair or two before it gets back to you AND

-More than two of your cards to improve to quads or a full house are gone.

Two Pair

As much as I love trips, I know there are times when I can get burned by them. Two pair is even more difficult. When I was a less experienced player, having two pair on fourth street terrified me, as this hand does many players. I've since learned to play it properly, but it still gives me a lot of anxiety. So you can avoid the difficulty I've had in these situations, I'm now going to teach you how to play this troublesome hand. As with trips, the key will be looking for reasons not to play this hand aggressively or to muck it before it gets you into trouble.

When I was new to the game, two pair was usually an automatic call for me, because I really had no idea how to play the hand. I did not want to fold, since I thought I had a decent chance to get a full house. At the same time, I didn't want to raise, because I really did not feel all that comfortable with the hand. It seemed too mediocre of a hand to win with. So, "just call," I would tell myself. But "just calling" with this hand, as tempting as it is to do, is often a big mistake.

When to Play and When to Run

Here's the first rule when you have two pair: you do not want to play the hand if more than one of your cards to improve is gone and there are other pairs on the board bigger than yours. If all four of your cards to fill up are live, you are still an underdog (3.5 to 1) to get a full house. Those odds certainly won't improve as play progresses.

If more than two of your cards are gone, it is *crucial* that you have a great two pair – jacks up or better. With anything less than that and more than two cards needed to fill up gone, the odds are against you unless the board looks very weak. Just limp in cheaply so you can get to fifth street if there is no higher pair on the board, and fold if there is a lot of action.

When you see that your cards are live and decide to play two pair, different situations will determine whether you bang away or just limp in. Let's say you're in middle or early position. If someone bets two dollars, a raise would be ideal with your two pair (provided no higher pairs have yet to bet), because other players yet to act will have to call two bets as opposed to just one, and they will be more apt to fold.

In late position, even if you do raise, most players will want to see fifth street, so it is much more likely that the drawing and marginal hands will stick around despite your raise. When their money is in the pot, they won't let a raise scare them off. Still, you should raise in late position if you believe you can get some players to drop – getting even one player out means one fewer player who can outdraw you.

Bigger is Always Better

If you're playing two pair, you want always to go into the hand with the belief that you hold the best hand. If you see *any* pair on the board that is higher than your two pair, fold unless you can get a free card. You very well may have that person beat if he has only one pair that is higher than yours, but with three cards yet to come, any smaller pair that he gets gives him a better two pair than you if you don't fill up. If it is the minimum bet or one bet to you and all of your cards are live, a call sometimes can be justified to see fifth street (if you must gamble), but calling will usually just cost you more money in the long run.

If you're considering sticking around, and there is a lot of action by the time the betting gets to you, a fold is a no-brainer. Never play into a bigger two pair if you don't have to! If a bigger pair has bet and another bigger pair is yet to act, even calling the minimum is a bad move, since a raise is highly likely from the big pair to your left. In sum, if you're staying in at all when there's a bigger pair on the board, limp in as cheaply as possible, and make sure every one of your cards to improve is live. More often than not, though, you should fold and be done with it.

When to Call

Playing two pair is clearly difficult, but as you can see you almost always have to choose between two extremes: play this hand hard or don't play it at all. Raise to make drawing hands pay, or fold if other hands seem stronger than yours. That said, there are also a few instances when you should just call. One is if it is two bets to you (eight dollars in a $2/4 game) and your two pair is *big* and *live*. Normally, you certainly do not want just to call with a big, live two pair, but a reraise from a player to your right to that high an amount on fourth street indicates that he has a very strong hand, probably trips. That being the case, when you have a good two pair and all live cards, call to see fifth street, but do not raise.

I should note that a situation such as this is pretty rare in low-limit stud. Normally, it will either be the minimum or maximum bet to you, but no more than the maximum unless it is a very aggressive table. If it is either the minimum or maximum bet to you, raise to let people know you have something.

In a perfect world, you would win the pot then and there. In low-limit stud, with so many calling stations, several players will stay in, but, in most games, several players yet

bably won't bring
but raise once the
 the best hand.

vith a big pair at
u might have the
 want to stay in,
g just to limp in
re saving money if
ng small is costing
yers aren't having
ply and probably

esirable, but there
. One such situa-
u. If it is just the
on the board, you
in for two dollars
raise is a probably
r hand. As long as
l hope to improve

there is a pair on
see any pair bigger
way. With just one
on the board, you
pair on the board
u have a good read

to act would also drop out. That's exactly what you want them to do so they don't get lucky down the line, catch a needed card, and cost you money.

Calling is also justified when you feel that a raise has no chance to knock out any other player. Look at an example. You are in late position, a pair of queens bet the mini-mum, but only one person called. A raise to four dollars is not likely to knock out the queens or the other caller. So you just call.

Going with your gut instincts is okay, too, if you don't feel raising is appropriate. Let's say an opponent with a pair of deuces brings it in for the full amount or raises it to four dollars — that player is probably trying to protect a two pair or trips, so it would be fine just to call if you know him to be tight-aggressive.

Never Play Scared
The one thing you cannot do with two pair is play scared. It *will* cost you. Yes, it may seem expensive to raise with two pair when it's not as powerful as you'd like it to be, but the fewer players in, the better for you. With live cards and a big two pair like aces up, never worry about raising even a big bet from a player who looks weaker than you — get those other players out of there.

Don't Forget Those Dead Cards
A final note on playing two pair: never forget which cards are live and which ones are dead. When more than two cards that would improve your two pair to a full house are

gone, you must always proceed with extreme c
ther muck the hand or play it hard and hope th
force out other players and win right there. If
that your raise will not force out many player
are only two cards left in the deck that can hel
unless you have other outs, such as three to a f
fall into the trap of hoping for the miracle card
the odds to be on your side when playing two

Quick Guide...

...to Two Pair on Fourth Stre

• **RAISE** when you have a big two pair high
anything that you can see on the board, un
two big bets back to you.
• **CALL** when you believe that a raise
force out other players or if your instinct te
player may have something big.
• **FOLD** when you have a weak two pair th
nerable to a higher pair on the board, unl
cards are all live. Folding is also best wh
than two cards that would improve the h
boat are dead.

Big Pairs

In many instances, you will have stayed in t
street with a big pair that did not improve or
card. Most of these times, unless more than
cards are gone and there's a lot of action (ind
bigger hands have been made by the time it

surprise them on the showdown. Y
it in with two weak cards on the b
action comes to you if you feel yo

It can be very tempting to bet s
fourth street, even when you thi
best hand at that time. Of cours
but without a great hand, it's te
until you improve. It may look lik
you don't improve your hand, but
you in the long-run because oth
to spend much. They're staying i
outdrawing you more times than

When to Limp In

Betting big with a pair on the boar
are also times when just calling is
tion is when it is a big bet back
minimum to you, and there's no
will want to raise. But if it is bro
and raised to four, don't re-raise –
an indication of a two pair or even
most of your cards are live, just ca
on fifth street.

Another situation in which to call
the board. With two pair, if you do
than yours exposed, you want to ba
pair, even if it's bigger than anyth
can't be certain that the player wit
hasn't made two pair. If you feel tha

on your opponent, perhaps you know him to be the kind of player who will only bet the maximum if he has two pair or better. In that case, if he limps in, raise to the maximum with your bigger pair to force out weaker hands. Most of the time, though, if there is a pair on the board, just call to see fifth street cheaply.

Mucking the Hand

With two pair, if you saw a bigger pair on the board, folding was the best decision unless every one of your cards was live. With just one pair, even if it is big, get out of there if you see that someone has made a bigger pair. For example, let's say you have a pair of jacks, and at this point you're clearly beaten by a player who has made a pair of aces. Unless you know that his other two aces are dead, fold. Going up against a bigger pair that clearly has you beaten here will just cost you money in the long run.

The only time you can consider calling is if your pair is hidden. Earlier in this section, I touched on the value that a hidden pair can have for you when you get to the showdown: a player won't see trips – or, better yet, a full house – coming. With a hidden pair in the same situation, you can call up to one big bet if most of your cards are live.

Don't Forget Those Kickers

During the discussion of third street play, I mentioned that the importance of a good kicker can never be underestimated. The same holds true here at fourth street, and the size of your kickers will play a large part in determining whether you call or fold. Let's look at an example to illustrate this point. Suppose you have pocket jacks. With no pair on the board, you'll be raising if it's one small bet to you. With a pair on the board, you'll be calling. What if someone holds a pair of queens to your right, and he just brought it in for the maximum? Certainly, you're gone if more than one of the cards you need to improve are gone. But before you reach for your chips or start to fold up your cards to muck them, look at your kickers.

Suppose you are holding a split pair of jacks, with a 10 for your other hole card and a king dealt to you on fourth street. In that case, assuming you haven't seen more than two dead cards, go ahead and call to see fifth street. You have possibilities for what could improve to trips, two pair, or even an open-ended straight draw. Now suppose you have the same split pair with lousy kickers. In that case, fold. Sure, the jacks look good, but you can already see that you are beat by a pair of queens. Never start out having to improve if you don't have to.

Quick Guide...
...to *Big Pairs* on *Fourth Street*
• **RAISE** with a big pair (especially if it's hidden) when you see no other pairs on the board and when you are confident that you have the best hand.
• **CALL** if it has been raised to you or if you see another pair on the board, unless you believe that your opponent is just trying to scare people off.
• **FOLD** when you see that a bigger pair has been made.

FOURTH STREET

Middle and Small Pairs

When you make a small or middle pair, most of the time, unless you've improved it at fourth street, you will be folding. There are a few times, though, when you will play to see fifth street. I'll mention those now, so you don't automatically fold when your middle pair does not improve.

Low-limit stud tends to be very passive at times, so you will often get to see fifth street cheaply. You can therefore play a medium or small pair more often at the low limits. But even if you can play the hand for one small bet, proceed with caution. Let's look at an example.

Say you have pocket 5s, with a jack and king on the board. It's one small bet to you, and you do not see anything to be too concerned about on the board. Unless your two other 5s are gone, or a 5 and one of your kickers are gone, you can call here. In the same situation, if there are some hands yet to act that look threatening – such as an open big pair – fold, unless you know that the player yet to act is so passive that he won't be raising with his big pair.

Another time you should call with a medium or little pair is when you hold three to a flush or straight. The odds are against your making either of these hands, but if no more than two of your cards to improve a pair are dead, call a minimum bet.

Kickers & Live Cards

I've said it time and time again, but I'll say it here, too. You must remember that one of the most important things to keep in mind before calling with a small or medium pair is the status of your live cards and kickers.

In that last example (5 5 J K), you have a decent hand because your kickers are good. If you had 5 5 8 2, that's a much more mediocre hand. You have to think long and hard about calling. I would call a minimum bet with the good kickers. If three of the cards were of the same suit and no more than two of the cards needed to improve the hand were dead, I'd even call up to one big bet. With the lousy kickers, it's best to fold (unless, of course, you can see fifth street for free).

Quick Guide...
...to *Middle and Small Pairs* on *Fourth Street*
• **CALL** a minimum bet if you have three-to-a-flush, three-to-a-straight, or a pair with good kickers and no more than two cards needed to improve dead.
• **FOLD** if it is a big bet or more back to you.

Flush and Straight Draws

Knowing when you should stay in with flush and straight draws comes down to being aware of live cards and the quality of your hand. In this section, we'll look at how to play four to a flush or straight. We'll also discuss when it's justifiable to stay in with three to a flush or straight.

FOURTH STREET

Three Flushes

With three to a flush, you're looking to stay in as cheaply as possible. In a perfect world, you would get a free card. In reality, most of the time you'll have to call at least one bet. If it is a big bet, fold the hand unless you have a good pair to go with your drawing hand. You can call a small bet, but only when you have a lot of live cards and good overcards.

Suppose that you hold J♥K♥A♦8♥. Three of your cards here are of the same suit, and it's one small bet back to you. Now, the odds are not too good that you'll hit a flush by the river – they're about 8.5 to 1. You can stick around, though, because you have some very good big cards that could improve on fifth street.

When you're deciding whether to call the bet, you'll want to look at who is yet to act. If you see an open pair of 9s or better, you must fold. Yes, it is only one small bet, but you have to be thinking that the holder of that pair very well may raise. If you don't see any other pairs on the board and nothing else looks too threatening (such as A-K suited) it's okay to call.

Note that if you call, you'll want to have a lot of live cards – kickers *and* cards of your suit. Because the odds are stacked against your making a flush, no more than two of the cards of your suit should be gone, and no more than two of the cards that would make your high kickers into pairs should be gone. Let's illustrate this using the above example. You have three to a heart flush and two high kickers. If two hearts are gone and all the aces and jacks are live, call. If a jack is gone and only one heart is gone, call. If four clubs and an ace are all gone, you must be gone, too. It's simply not worth the risk – save your chips for when you do have something that can make people pay.

Four Flushes

Your decision is much easier when you have four to a flush on fourth street. Whenever you are fortunate enough to have four to a flush, you'll probably be sticking around to see the very last card. But there are some exceptions.

It's natural to be excited when you hold four to a flush on fourth street. Surely the fifth card will fall, right? Yes, your odds are good, but before you automatically call every bet from here on, realize that there are times when you should lay down your four-flush. Mucking this hand is very, very difficult, especially when it's been a long time since you've seen a hand. But you have to know when to fold it. Granted, the vast majority of the time you'll play this hand, but you'll still have to lay it down every so often.

With all drawing hands, it's ideal to be in late position. It's a great asset to know how much action has taken place by the time the betting gets to you. If it's two big bets back to you, as tough as it is to do so, fold. This would usually occur only when there is more than one good pair on the board. For example, a pair of queens brings it in for four dollars, and a pair of jacks on the board raises. Now it's eight dollars to you. Sure, you are fairly likely to complete your hand by the river, but with two big bets to you, it's also likely that at least one of the players who has bet has trips. A flush beats trips, but with trips at fourth street, your opponent has a great shot to fill up. In a situation like this, fold unless you are on a straight-flush draw, in which case you can call.

From time to time, you can mix up your play and consider a raise or a bet if there has been no action and you are in late position. Suppose you are last to act and it has been checked to you. If you bet two dollars here, even though you don't have your hand right now, you may buy yourself a free card on fifth street, as players may check to you. This will help you if you don't make your flush at fifth street. Raising also allows you to mix up your play, so players won't assume you are always on a draw when you have two suited cards on the board. It's especially good to do this if you often play with the same people.

Live Card Requirements

Live cards are always a must, but just how many need to be live on a flush or straight draw? There is no set rule, but if I have a flush draw with several face cards and I'm facing a big bet, I want no more than four cards to be dead. If my four-flush has smaller cards, I'll want no more than three of my suit dead. In late position or with no chance of a raise and facing just one small bet, you can be slightly more liberal in your requirements. With big cards, you can stay with up to five dead cards; with smaller ones, you can stay with up to four.

With four of the same suit your hand may look pretty, but it's worthless without that fifth card to complete it. When more than five cards are gone, there are only four cards left in the deck that can help you. The dead cards of your suit aren't going to re-appear until the next hand, when they won't do you much good. So with more than five cards to complete your flush gone, fold.

Three-to-a-Straight

Earlier, I mentioned that I really do not like straight draws. I didn't like them on third street, and if I haven't improved, I certainly don't like them on fourth street. It's just fine not to play these hands – I'll rarely play three to a straight that hasn't improved on fourth street, unless I can see fifth street for free.

Can this hand be played at all? The answer is: only in rare circumstances. One is, of course, that you want your cards to be big. Even with big cards, if you don't catch a card on fourth street that improves your straight draw, the odds are now 10 to 1 against your making a straight by the river. Not good.

Can you ever play a straight draw on fourth street that has not improved much from third? The only time you can even consider doing so is if your draw did improve to a "gutshot" or inside straight draw, all of the cards to complete the straight are live, the cards are big, *and* you could get in for one minimum bet. All of that is *not* going to happen very often. And even when it does happen, you must play an inside straight draw *very* selectively.

FOURTH STREET

Let's say you have 9 10 J, and with fourth street comes a king. You now have an inside straight draw, and it's one small bet to you. If there is nothing threatening yet to act, it's okay to call. If you do see a big pair yet to bet, even limping in isn't worth it. Odds are that you'll have to go up against a raise from the big pair.

With smaller straight draws that have not improved, fold most of the time. Unless you are playing hi-lo split stud poker, they aren't worth chasing. Again, anytime you consider seeing fifth street with an inside straight draw, *all* of the cards you need to complete the hand must be live. Never confuse this hand with a flush draw – there you have more cards that can help you. When only four cards in the deck can complete your hand, with even one gone, the odds, which are already against you, only grow worse.

Don't Forget Those Odds...

Speaking of the odds, when you're trying to figure out whether to stay in with an inside straight draw, keep in mind the odds the pot is giving you. When you have four cards to a straight, and you're on an inside straight draw, the odds of getting that needed card are 3 to 1 – assuming that all your cards are live. Suppose the pot has $15 dollars in it, and it's one small bet to you. To call, you'd be putting a $2 bet into a $15 dollar pot, which would give you odds of greater than 3 to 1. Thus, because the pot odds here outweigh the general odds of hitting your hand, you can go ahead and call. This is a good bet to make, assuming your cards are live.

Open-Ended Straight Draws

When you have four cards to an open-ended straight, you will usually go ahead and play this hand as long as possible. Of course, an open-ended straight draw with four cards is much better than three to a straight. The odds are now pretty good – about 1.5 to 1 – that you will make a straight by the river. Still, as with a four-flush, don't automatically be calling every bet and assuming that the card you need to complete your hand will fall.

So when can you call? One instance is when the board does not look too threatening. Be on guard if you see one or two big pairs – you certainly do not want to make your straight and have it beaten by a full house later on.

You must also proceed with caution if there's a lot of action before the betting gets to you. You never want to call if it's more than one big bet to you. You may have a good shot to make the straight, but even with live cards, more than one big bet on fourth street means at least one of the players has a very good hand. Your straight won't hold up against a flush or better. Fortunately, most of the time at the low limits, there won't be a lot of banging away on fourth street, so you can call. In many cases, you can even stay until the river with four to an open-ended straight.

Once again, you also need to consider how many of your cards are live. Requirements are slightly more liberal with flush draws, because the odds are slightly better for completing a four-flush than a four-straight, and a flush is a better hand. While the odds may be good to get a straight, you always have to remember that they are relative to how many cards are live. Ideally, all of your cards to complete your straight are live, but that's not often the case.

How many cards can be dead? With an open-ended straight draw, you should rarely play with more than two cards gone if you're facing one big bet. You should rarely play with more than three cards gone if you're facing one small bet. Staying in for a minimum bet is okay with three cards, but you want to make sure when you do that you have big cards – such as a 9 10 J Q hand – to go along with your straight draw. As a rule of thumb, though, with more than three cards to complete your straight gone, do not give in to temptation to call and call. You will just be giving away your money.

Quick Guide...
...to *Flush and Straight Draws* on *Fourth Street*
- **RAISE** rarely – only if you have four to a straight flush, with a lot of live cards.
- **CALL** when you have four to a flush and no more than five of the cards needed to complete it are dead, or when you have four to a straight and no more than three of the cards needed to complete it are dead. Remember, in both cases, the bigger the better. Call a three-flush or three-straight if you have big cards or a pair and can limp in cheaply.
- **FOLD** if too many of your needed cards are gone or if there is a lot of heavy betting before the action gets to you.

Fourth Street: A Summary

This ends our discussion of play on fourth street. From here on, action will begin to pick up. The betting will always be the maximum, so you will have to exercise caution, but when you do play, you'll be playing aggressively. As play goes along, it is crucial to start out strong if you want to get stronger. At third and fourth street, the bets are frequently inexpensive – with the loose/passive nature of many low-limit games, it's common to go long periods of time with no raises to the maximum.

By this point, you should see that you clearly should *not* be one of those passive players when you have something! When you do get a good hand, play it hard and aggressive. But never, ever fall into the trap of playing loosely just to see the fifth card, as some players do. Granted, the betting is not as heavy yet as it will be once we get to fifth street, but if you stay in time and time again with mediocre cards, you will just be giving away money. A dollar here, a small bet there, and it will add up over a session. Be patient! The good cards will come, and when they do you want to be in a position to make a good hand great, so you'll be all smiles at the showdown.

Quick Quiz: Fourth Street

To review and test your knowledge, take the following quick quiz. Then let's move on to fifth street, where the action picks up and the bets increase.

Questions

1. In middle position, you hold a split pair of 10s and two medium kickers. One of your 10s is dead. A player with an ace and king showing on the board bets two dollars, and a pair of 5s on the board raises the betting to four dollars. It's now one big bet to you. You know that no other 5s are dead. Do you fold, call or raise?

2. You hold two pair, queens and 5s. One of your 5s is dead. There is one small pair on the board, and, since your queens are showing on the board, you are first to act. Do you bring it in for the minimum or the maximum?

3. You had a split pair of 5s on third street which didn't improve on fourth street. Three of your cards are suited, however, and you have two good kickers: an ace and a queen. Only one queen is dead, and you haven't seen many of your suit on the board. Your 5s are also live. You're in middle position, it's one small bet to you, and there is nothing too threatening on the board – just a small pair, who bet the minimum. Do you fold, call or raise?

4. You limped in with a split pair of deuces on third street, and it's now improved to trips. Your other card is a king, and while all the kings are still live, the other deuce has been dealt to another player. You're in late position, and it is one big bet to you – a small pair bet two dollars and was raised by a player with a jack and a 10 on the board. There was one other caller. Do you raise or call?

5. You started out with three-to-a-flush, but the fourth card brought no help. You've seen four of your suit fall to other players. You have an ace as a high card, but the rest of your cards are relatively small. You are in early position, and while there are no pairs on the board, the player who bet ahead of you bet the minimum. Do you call?

6. You started out by limping in with three-to-a-straight: a 5, a 6, and a 7. A trey is dealt to you on fourth street. You've seen one 4 fall. You are in middle position, and a pair of 9s bets four dollars. There are several callers, including another small pair. Do you call?

7. You started out with three-to-a-straight, and you haven't improved. You do have several big cards – a jack, queen and king – and only one queen is dead. You are in late position, and the board looks weak with no pairs. An ace-high has bet two dollars to you. Do you stay in?

8. You started with a three-flush that's improved to a four-flush. Three of the cards of your suit have fallen. You're in late position, and you face one big bet – the small bet was raised by an open pair of 10s. There have been two callers, and you'd be the fifth person in the pot. Do you stay in?

9. You have a small four-straight. Only one of your cards is dead, and your straight is open-ended. A pair of aces brought in the betting for four dollars, and it was promptly raised by a pair of queens. Do you stay in?

10. You limped in as the bring-in bet on third street, but you had three big cards – a 10, a queen, and an ace. Now you've got a 9. The board looks weak, and when it comes to you, it's just one small bet. Do you call or fold?

Answers

1. Fold. One of your 10s is already dead, your kickers are not of good quality, and a raise from the pair of 5s is a good indicator that the player has probably improved to two pair or possibly trips. Calling one small bet would be okay, but you don't want to call a full bet with those lousy kickers and a dead 10.

2. Bet the maximum. You could be up against trips from the small pair, but your concern is to protect your two pair. It's a good hand, but you'd like to win even if your hand does not improve. Bet the full amount, and make other players who are on draws think long and hard about staying in. Ideally, you'll be heads up against the player who has the smaller pair. If not, at least you'll cut the field.

3. Call. You're an underdog to make a flush, but several things are working in your favor here – good kickers, live cards to improve to trips, and a three-flush. Calling even one big bet is justifiable here given your good overcards, but any more than that and you would have to fold.

4. Raise. Don't feel too uncomfortable about doing so, even if it's a big bet to you. Your goal is to narrow the field as much as possible. If you're re-raised, just call, but with a hand as good as trips after your fourth card, protect it. You want to win with just that, in case you don't fill up.

5. Fold. Muck this hand. Too many cards of your needed suit are already gone, and you have mediocre kickers. Facing high odds and having poor kickers, don't try to beat the odds. The pot is too small right now to be giving you good pot odds, so fold and wait for the better hand.

6. Fold. Calling with live cards would be okay if your straight were open-ended, but because you are on a guts-hot (inside) straight draw here, fold. There are only three cards in the deck that can help you, and with a small, low-quality straight, it's not worth sticking around.

7. Call. It is just one small bet, you have big cards, and because you are in late position, you've had the chance to see what the other players have done. Go ahead and stick around in hopes that you'll get another card to your straight draw, or perhaps a big pair.

8. Call. Ideally, the bigger your cards are the better, but with four-to-a-flush on fourth street, you have a great shot to make the flush.

9. Fold. You may have a great shot to make your straight, but a straight isn't going to win this pot. The players may have just two pair or trips (which a straight will beat), but with three cards yet to come, they have a great shot to beat you. Save yourself the eight dollars.

10. Fold. This is a trap, and it's easy to fall into it. It's only two bucks, and the board looks lousy, so why not stay in, right? Wrong! Staying in will cost you money. You have a few big cards, but you want three-to-a-flush or straight even to consider limping in. Fold the hand and wait until you get a pair or better drawing possibility.

5

FIFTH STREET

Whether to proceed with the hand at third street is the most important decision you will make in a single hand. A close second, however, is whether you want to continue past the fifth card (fifth street). What makes this portion of the game so significant? The answer is in the betting.

On previous rounds, you could place just a small bet. Once you hit fifth street, all bets must be for the maximum amount. The game becomes more expensive, and once you make a decision to stay in at fifth street, it's likely that you'll be staying all the way to the end. So by this point, you want either to have made your hand or to feel that you have a very strong possibility of completing the hand.

Because the game gets more expensive at fifth street, it's extremely important to know when you should stay in till the end. It's also crucial to know when you want to play aggressively to make it very expensive for marginal drawing hands to stay in the pot. In this chapter, we'll look at which hands you must have to stay in at fifth street and how you should play them. We'll start with the bigger hands and then finish up with the drawing hands.

The Monster Hands

Nothing is better than having made a powerful hand that you're convinced has no chance of losing. So what constitutes a "monster hand?" The best way to define it is as a very powerful hand that will very rarely be beaten. A straight flush, quads, or a big full house constitutes such a hand.

When you're playing a monster hand, take your foot off of the accelerator. Yes, you should play aggressively when you are trying to force out drawing hands, but with a huge hand you do not want them to be out of the way. Instead, when you have made a huge hand, ease up at first to see what other players will do. You know you'll have a big surprise waiting for them by the time you get to the last card, so let them stay in. Set a trap.

As tempting as it is to raise or re-raise in these situations, with a monster hand you want to let the other players draw dead to their hands, so you win a huge pot. In the best scenario, your opponents will complete their flushes or straights, and they'll let you raise and re-raise them by the time sixth and seventh streets roll around.

Raising With a Monster

Is it ever okay on fifth street to raise and re-raise with a monster hand? Certainly. For instance, if there are not many players left, and you believe the players left will not fold, even with a lot of action, go ahead and raise a player's bet. Remember, though, when you have a monster hand, the more players that are in the pot, the better. Another instance in which it's best to raise the bet is when you are in late position and there's been a lot of action by the time it comes to you. Putting more money in the pot won't scare off those who have already bet and raised – they simply will call your raise. They want to stay in until the end.

Finally, although you want to call most of the time with great hands such as quads or a big full house, you don't want to do so all of the time. Unlike in hold 'em poker, in stud, you can never be certain when you have the absolute **nuts** – a hand that can't be beaten. If you believe there is any chance that one of your opponents has something better than what you hold, go ahead and raise.

Quick Guide...
...to *Monster Hands* on *Fifth Street*
• **RAISE** if there has been a lot of action (two bets or more) by the time the betting gets to you.
• **CALL** most of the time, so others can build your pot – you'll have time to raise on sixth or seventh street.

Playing a Full House

Few things are more exciting than catching two pair and then having the poker gods bless you with the magical card that completes your hand to a full house. A boat is a huge hand in any poker game, and the vast majority of the time it will win you a decent-sized pot. Nonetheless, just because it is a great hand does not mean that it should be played the same way every single time. There are two typical ways to play a full house – either you can bang away with it, or you can slow-play it. Let's look at both.

Banging Away

In most cases, you will bang away whenever you have a boat. I mentioned the most common exception to this rule in the previous section – slow-playing a big full house can be a great idea. The keyword to that rule is *big*. What do I mean by a "big" full house? I mean that you want your full house to be bigger than any potential full house you see on the board. Never, ever, slow-play your boat if you see a pair that could become a bigger boat than yours.

For example, let's say you have jacks full of 9s – a huge hand. But, on the board, you see an open pair of queens. That player has bet, and now the betting is to you. Your first instinct should not be to call in this situation – doing so can cost you money. Unless both of the other queens are dead, raise. You want to try to force this opponent out so he won't fill up and beat you with a bigger full house.

The odds are still with you to win the hand, but if there is ever a higher pair than your full house, bang away to make its holder pay. Raising is also the right thing to do if an opponent has a few big cards in front of him. If an opponent had A K J on the board against your jacks full, granted, he doesn't have an open pair, but with three big cards like that, two could represent a pair that, with improvement, could fill up to a bigger boat than yours. In such an instance, you should raise.

Sandbagging

Calling on fifth street with a full house is fine if your boat is big and the only pairs you see on the board are smaller that what you have in your hand. In fact, calling is the best move. Get your opponents to stay in – your hope is that they will fill up to smaller full houses than yours, which will result in a lot of action in later betting rounds. That will pay you off nicely. Also call when you see a lot of probable flush and straight draws on the board. Even if they make their hands, you already have them beat. Don't worry about trying to force them out now. Rather, let them pay you off once you get to the showdown.

Finally, should you ever *fold* a full house on fifth street? Very rarely. The only instance when folding might cross your mind is if you see trips on the board that would represent a full house bigger than yours. For instance, suppose you again hold those jacks full of 9s, and there are three aces open on the board. Ouch. By the time it gets to you, odds are it will be just one bet – the bet from the open aces. No one would raise him. With a full house, you generally want to call – the player would have to have the last ace or a pair in the hole to be full.

If, however, the player played aggressively on third street, the three-of-a-kind on the board might be an indicator that he has more than the trips on the board – quad aces or aces full. If that's the case – and such a situation is quite rare – knowing your opponent well will help you determine whether to fold your full house. Doing so is very, very difficult, and with a full house, even when there are greater trips on the board, calling is the best thing to do, especially if the last card that would improve you to quads is still alive. The only time I would recommend folding a boat on fifth street is if you've seen a lot of heavy action (two bets or more) by the time the betting gets to you from hands that could be better than your full house.

Here's an example: let's say I have 4s full of 9s. A player with trip 7s on the board has bet, and he has been re-raised by a pair of kings on the board. It's two bets back to me. The little voice inside of me may say to call, but with two bets before me from two hands that could have me beaten, the right move would be to fold. Doing this will take you a lot of discipline. Fortunately, though, the situation won't come up all that often. When it does, having the courage to lay down a great hand will save you money, and you'll be breathing a big sigh of relief come the showdown.

Quick Guide...
...to a Full House on Fifth Street

• **RAISE** with a full house that's 9s full or worse. Raise if you see any pairs that could improve to a full house bigger than yours. Finally, always re-raise if it is two bets to you and you do not see anything threatening from the player who raised.

• **CALL** if you have a big full house and there are clearly no other threats.

• **FOLD** *rarely* with a full house, but do so if you feel that you are beaten by a player who has already made a bigger hand than yours.

FIFTH STREET

Completed Flushes & Straights

When we looked at how to play monster hands, I emphasized that you should play slowly, so as to keep as many people as possible in the pot. When you complete a straight or a flush on fifth street, you may be tempted just to call all bets that come your way. After all, you've made a good hand, so just keep those players in so they can pay you off, right?

Wrong! You should rarely play a flush or straight slowly. As a rule, you want to play these hands as aggressively and as hard as possible, unless you find a compelling reason not to. If you play the hand passively (just call bets that come your way), you'll be letting people with drawing hands stay in cheaply. They may draw to a bigger straight, flush or full house and win a hand that you should have won.

When Calling is Okay

I've said that the vast majority of flushes and straights need to be played very aggressively, but there are cases when you will want just to call bets. Look for a reason not to play the hand hard. Although you will be raising with a straight or flush at fifth street most of the time, there are those instances when calling will be the best thing to do. Let's look at those situations now.

During our discussion of playing a full house, you saw that calling was the right decision when it was two big bets back to you and there was something on the board that could have you beaten, such as bigger trips. Keep this same rule in mind when you play a completed flush or straight. If you see something to indicate that a player has already made a hand that's bigger than yours, just call the bet rather than raise.

Here's an example: I hold a 10-high straight and am in late position. One player has bet and several others have called, so it's one bet back to me. Before automatically raising, I glance down at the bettor's open cards and see that he has three 7s on the board. My straight certainly can't beat a boat. Here, if I have a good knowledge of my opponent, and if I know him to be the type of player who would bet only if he had made his hand, I would fold. In most circumstances, though, I would call to see what he does on sixth street.

A raise might force out a drawing hand, but you need to know your opponent very well if you are considering raising his trips on the board. Most of the time, though, you'd just call his bet here. So what if he has just a pair on the board? Would calling be the right move?

Your first thought might be "yes," as the pair could represent a completed full house. But you should not let a pair intimidate you unless a player with a pair on the board raises a big bet that comes to him. If he simply bets, go ahead and raise. The odds are that he probably hasn't filled up yet. It's likely he's trying to defend his two pair or trips to force people out, so make it costly for him to stick around.

Even if he does stay, your raise will force out other players, which will be a good thing for you. Do not let a three-flush or three-straight bigger than yours spook you – the player still needs two more cards, so bang away and don't let him get those two cards cheaply. You've got your hand already, so protect it.

When to Fold

Are there times when you will fold a flush or straight at fifth street? As with a full house, these times will be few and far between. Most often you might have to fold a straight. The only time you should fold a completed flush or straight is when there seems to be overwhelming evidence that another player has you beaten. Let's return to the example of a 10-high straight. A player with three diamonds on the board bets, and trip 7s raises him. All the other players fold, so it's now two big bets back to you. Here you have to think long and hard about sticking around.

You can stay in with a flush (so long as your highest card is higher than the highest card on the board). A straight is not a bad hand at all and will frequently win the pot, but it won't win this one when you are up against two players who could have better hands. Fold and wait for a bigger hand, so that when it does come your way, you'll have plenty of chips with which to bet. Of course, with no trips on the board, and if you're up against just the three diamonds, you want to raise unless you know your opponent to be a very tight player who will bet only when he has made his hand.

CARDOZA PUBLISHING • KAMMEN

> ## Quick Guide...
> ### ...to *Flushes and Straights* on *Fifth Street*
> • **RAISE** unless you find a strong reason not to – you want to play this hand hard and try to win the pot right here.
> • **CALL** if you feel that a player might have you beaten but you aren't certain.
> • **FOLD** rarely – only if it looks like you are clearly beaten.

Trips

When they haven't improved their trips to quads or a full house at fifth street, some players who are passive have more of a tendency just to call. This was a problem for me when I first started playing. I was certainly happy to have trips, but there was that nervous voice inside of me that told me just to call, bet cautiously, and wait until I got my full house before playing aggressively.

The fact is that playing that way will cost you money. You have two cards to come, and the odds are not bad that you will end up with a full house – about 2.5 to 1. But, just like with flushes and straights, you want to play this hand as hard as possible to force out hands that could threaten you if you don't improve your hand. You cannot be thinking, "I will improve." Instead you must be thinking, "I want to win with this even if I don't improve."

One thing that can be intimidating for players with trips is a bigger pair or two on the board. Say you're holding trip 9s, and a pair of jacks on the board bets. Another player calls, and he has a three-flush on the board. That cautious voice inside of you may say "Uh-oh, a flush and a bigger set of trips...better just call." Don't listen to that voice. Odds are that you have both of these players beat – so raise. At the very least, raising will force out other players. It may also make the original bettors think twice about deciding to proceed with the hand.

Raising may even win you the pot there, and you will be able to relax a little (though most of the time the raise will not drive off the original bettor). But it will at least narrow the field, which will benefit you much more than having a number of players stick around who can outdraw you. Always try to minimize your competition, especially when other players have bigger pairs than you do. Don't let their bets intimidate you into calling – make them pay to play!

Calling

As with straights and flushes, most of the time you will raise with trips. You want to force out drawing hands. Should you *ever* call with trips? It will be very rare, but it can happen. One instance is when it is two bets back to you, indicating that someone has improved to a full house or flush. Because you have trips and have a good shot at getting a full house by the river, call, unless you see that a lot of cards to improve the hand are already dead.

Let's say you hold trip 9s, and a player with a three-flush

bets. He is raised by a pair of 5s on the board. Now it's two bets back to you. Just call here. The raise from the 5s will do the job of driving out the more marginal hands, thus narrowing the field to you and the other two players. Even though you may be going up against a full house and/or a flush, you have a good shot to improve your hand to a full house. That would beat both other hands, so to stick around until the end.

Folding

As with the hands we discussed previously (a full house, a straight, and a flush) folding with trips at fifth street is highly unlikely. But it may happen that you have to fold. One instance where the decision to fold isn't too hard is when there is an open set on the board that's bigger than yours. For instance, with trip 7s, if you see a set of trip 9s on the board, why on earth stick around? This player has you beaten, so folding here is a no-brainer.

Another instance in which folding is the best decision is when you find that a lot of the cards (more than three) you'd need to improve the hand to quads or a full house are dead, and it's two bets back to you. With a lot of action and not a lot of cards that can help you, it's best to fold your trips. More than three cards you need are already gone, so the odds aren't in your favor to improve. Why go up against a potentially made bigger hand when there are few cards that will help you? Just fold.

Quick Guide...
...to *Trips* on *Fifth Street*

• **RAISE** most of the time – make opponents with drawing hands pay to play.

• **CALL** if it is two bets to you and it looks like someone else has something threatening, such as a made flush, a full house, or a bigger set of trips.

• **FOLD** if there is a bigger set of trips on the board or a lot of action from a three-flush or bigger pair and more than three of your cards are dead.

Two Pair

Playing two pair on fourth street certainly was not easy, and the comfort you have in playing this hand won't improve all that much on fifth street. There are, though, some pieces of advice I can give you to help you feel more comfortable in deciding whether to continue with this hand.

Of primary importance, of course, are live cards. You want many cards that you'd need to improve to a full house to be live. With more than two of those cards dead, just check if you can and fold if it comes back to you, unless you hold a powerful pair (such as aces or kings) on the board, and you're convinced you will win the pot or vastly narrow the field if you bet.

Another crucial factor in determining whether to proceed to sixth street with two pair is the size of your two pair.

Remember, you never want to play into a bigger two pair when you see one on the board – even with live cards. This is an important reminder, and it has saved me a lot of money. When there's a bigger pair on the board (assuming the other two cards to help that player are live) you want to fold and be done with the hand. You're an underdog to improve anyway, but you're even more of an underdog when you are going up against a probable two pair that is bigger than yours. Just fold and wait until you have the better hand.

On the flip side, if you are the player with a big two pair, don't be too intimidated by lower pairs. If no more than two of the cards you need to improve are dead, go ahead and bet (or even raise) if it's to you. The fewer players the better, and, ideally, you'd like to win the hand right here on fifth street.

Because of the change in the betting limits, a bet here may actually be more beneficial to you than it was at fourth street. Unless you had a pair on the board, you could bet only the minimum if no one had yet bet on fourth street. But here, because the limits have increased to the maximum, a bet from you is more likely to scare off players than it was before. So, with a strong two pair, force them out and narrow the field. You're hoping you will fill up, but if you don't, a strong two pair will frequently hold up as the number of players left decreases.

Playing two pair is very confusing and nerve-wracking. You have a good but not great hand. Playing it too passively is one of the most common mistakes that even otherwise solid stud players make. Despite my years of experience, even I am sometimes reluctant to play two pairs as hard as I should – but if you do so you will win more money than you will lose.

Laying down two pair can also be an incredibly difficult thing to do. After all, you need only one more card to fill up. That voice inside of you says, "Throw out those chips and let's go for it!" "Going for it" with weaker two pairs when there are indicators that your opponent could have you beaten or when there are too many dead cards will more often than not just result in your stack of chips disappearing quickly. Wait for those big two pairs with live cards, and when you get them, play them hard!

Quick Guide...
...to *Two Pair* on *Fifth Street*
- **RAISE** if you feel that you have the best hand, unless more than two of your cards are dead.
- **CALL** if you are in a game with loose opponents and you feel that a raise will be ineffective in driving them out.
- **FOLD** if you see a higher pair on the board than your two pair or if more than two of your cards to improve are gone.

Pairs

Folding two pair can be quite difficult, but folding a pair – especially a big pair – is no piece of cake either. For instance, let's say you start out with pocket aces, but then you get three lousy cards. So you tell yourself, "Hey, I've still got a good pair here – so I'll get that two pair or trips, and maybe I'll even fill up! I'm at a casino, so I might as well gamble, right?" Most of the time, the answer to that question ought to be "No!"

Many hands that start out great simply do not improve, and you must fold them. The majority of the time, in fact, this is a hand that you will fold. Still, there are some instances when you can proceed past fifth street with a pair, so folding should not be automatic. In this section, we'll look at the times that arise when you can play this hand.

When to Play
Of course, if it's no bet to you, you will be checking and hoping to get a free card. Beyond that, however, the biggest factor that goes into deciding whether to stay with this hand is position. You want all the cards you need to improve to trips to be live, very few players left, and good kickers. Again and again I have emphasized how much of an advantage it can be to be in late position. With a pair on fifth street, late position is especially useful.

As with two pair, the odds are better for you when there are fewer players in the pot. Ideally, if you're staying, only one or two players should be left. If there are a lot of drawing hands sticking around, just muck the hand. Unfortunately, since we are talking about the low limits in this book, in most instances three or more players will stick around to see sixth street, so more often than not you will be folding this hand. It is playable at times; those times, however, just do not come along too often.

Let's say that three or more players are sticking around, but, nevertheless, you decide that you desperately want to see sixth street. The *only* other instance when you can play a pair past fifth street is when you meet *all* of these three criteria:

> 1) You hold a big pair.
> 2) You have live cards.
> 3) You have overcards.

A hidden pair is also better than a split one. For instance, let's say you have pocket jacks and a king and an ace on the board. One player bets; three others call. If you must, call, but again, you want all of your cards to improve to trips to be live in this situation. Note that folding is a perfectly acceptable play in this situation. I would fold here unless I knew my opponents very well and knew them to be the types of players who would stay in with nothing.

Quick Guide...
...to *Pairs* on *Fifth Street*
• **CALL** if you have live cards and a very narrow field (no more than two other players).
• **FOLD** usually – unless you have a small field, a big pair, live cards *and* good over cards.

The Drawing Hands

Whenever you have four-to-a-flush or four-to-a-straight, it's quite easy to fall into the trap of having tunnel vision. Before you were more focused on closely following the moves of others and watching their cards. Now, being oh-so-close to the flush or straight, you may find yourself just staring at your hand as the dealer deals the fifth street card, waiting anxiously for the card to complete your hand. You may become oblivious to what other players are doing. A bet? You respond with a call. A raise? Another call on your part.

When drawing to a flush or straight at fifth street, there are many circumstances in which you should stay to the end. But *never* get tunnel vision. You need to be focused on all that goes on around you. Don't concern yourself with just the cards that you need. Obviously, your cards will be the primary factor that determines whether you keep or fold your hand, but other factors come into play, too. In this section, we'll look at those other factors, and I'll tell you when to stay and when to run away.

When to Stay

First, let's talk about sticking around. Again, this should be *anything* but an automatic move for you. Most of the time you will indeed be staying to see the last card, but not always. Again, live cards are your most important consideration. There is some leeway, but the point at which you need to fold a four-flush at fifth street is when six or more of your needed suit have fallen. If you're staying in with six of your needed suit dead, you must hold high cards or have other opportunities (such as a three-straight) to go along with your four-flush.

In any circumstance, though, fold when more than six of the cards to complete your flush are gone – unless you can see sixth street for free. Sure, there may be three cards left in the deck that can help you – but unlike when you're staying in with a pair or two pair, the difference here is that you currently have *nothing*.

A bunch of random cards is not going to get you much in regular stud poker. A bunch of low cards might get you a half-pot in hi-low split games, but that's not what we're playing here, so *always* fold your hand when more than six of your needed suit are dead, unless you can get a free card. If exactly six of your suit are dead, you can stick around if you have big cards that are live. The only other instance when sticking around is the right decision with more than six dead cards is when you have four to a straight flush. Here, with many outs, you'll want to be staying to the river.

Straight Draw Requirements

When we looked at straight draws before, I noted that the requirements were more stringent, since the flush is the bigger hand. The situation hasn't changed here. If more than three of the cards you need to complete an open-ended straight are gone, or if even one is gone to complete an inside straight, your best decision is to fold. The same exception applies as did with a flush draw – you can stay in if you have big, live cards or big cards that are three-to-a-flush.

Again, remember, that where your cards are concerned, the bigger the better. Don't hesitate to fold an open-ended straight if more than three of your needed cards are gone, and don't hesitate to fold an inside-straight if you have one dead card.

Don't Be the Chump
When it's more than one big bet to you, think long and hard about staying in the hand. In most of these situations, you should fold. Your folding has nothing to do with having the proper number of live cards or overcards. With two big bets, you have to figure that you are probably drawing to the second best hand. It's quite easy to fall into that trap, especially with a flush draw.

A flush is a great hand, but it's not going to look so great when your opponent turns over a full house at the showdown. You must keep that in mind when you're deciding whether to proceed with your flush and straight draws, and you must always ask yourself, "Am I just paying money to get the second-best hand?"

In my experience, I've found that, at the low limits, people don't re-raise too often at fifth street. The player with a monster hand will slow play to keep in other hands; the player with the good but not great hand is content just to call a bet when it comes his way, especially since it's now the maximum bet for the limit. But there are times when someone will re-raise. Because it's relatively rare to find low-limit players bluffing, when you hold a drawing hand, a re-raise should immediately set off warning bells in your head.

Most likely, a re-raise will come from a tight-aggressive player who is holding a completed hand; at times, it will come from a player holding trips. A flush will beat trips, but with two cards to come, his odds aren't that much worse than your odds to get your hand (for more details on odds, see the Appendix). Before you decide whether you can call two big bets, look carefully around the table and try to remember which cards are dead.

If you get a re-raise from a player who has J J 8 showing, you can figure him for trip jacks or possibly a full house. If you look around the board and see that two or more of the cards he needs to improve his hand are gone, and your hand meets the requirements to continue, you can proceed with the hand – the odds to complete the flush outweigh odds to complete a full house. However, even though you have good odds to complete your hand, fold if you see that his cards are live. It's just not worth spending that kind of money on a flush draw.

You may have noticed that I did not use straight draws in discussing what to do when you face two big bets. The reason is that if you hold four cards to a straight and there are two big bets back to you, unless the re-raise if from what looks to be a weaker straight, your hand must quickly be in the muck. A straight will lose to any better straight, any flush, or any full house. Your odds of completing your straight are the same as the odds of completing a flush, but with so many hands that can beat you, a re-raise signifies someone drawing to a better hand than yours or someone who already has a better hand than you do. So dump the hand.

Quick Guide...
...to *Drawing Hands* on *Fifth Street*
• **CALL** with a four-flush or four-straight when no more than five of the cards you need are dead.
• **FOLD** when more than five of the cards you need to complete your hand are gone. Consider a fold when it is two big bets back to you.

Fifth Street: A Summary
This brings us to the end of fifth street discussion. From here on, if you're in, you'll probably be in to the end. Before we move on, let's take a moment to review what we've covered.

By this point, I hope you've learned that you want to have stringent requirements before proceeding with a hand past fifth street. A great starting hand that hasn't improved often isn't worth chasing. On the flip side, a good hand at fifth street isn't worth playing passively when you believe it to be the best hand. Your goal is to win the pot – either by staying in cheaply while on a drawing hand, or by playing weaker made hands (such as trips) hard to force out the opponents who are trying to stay in cheaply. Don't let the increased betting levels scare you – use them to your advantage to play a good hand hard.

If you are a casual player, you may be thinking that the playing style described so far is very tight. Tight, yes. But aggressive, too. You have to pick and choose your hands carefully – especially when you get to fifth street, because the size of the betting increases at this level.

Quick Quiz: Fifth Street

Take the following quick quiz for review, and then let's move on to learn how to play your hand at sixth street.

Questions

1. You hold two pair – queens and 7s – and are in middle position. One 7 is dead, and on the board are a pair of 5s and a pair of 9s. The holder of the 9s bet four dollars. There were two callers, and now the action is to you. Do you raise or call?

2. You have a small two pair, 5s and deuces. Just one deuce is dead. You are in early position, second to bet after a pair of kings. The player with the kings bet four dollars. Of the players yet to act, the most threatening hands are a pair of 7s and a three to a flush. Do you call or fold?

3. You have four-to-a-flush, and you've seen four of your needed suit fall. You are in late position, and when a pair of 9s bet, several players called but none raised. Do you fold, call or raise?

4. You are in early position, and you hold four-to-a-straight. A pair of aces bets, and you call. A pair of 10s raises it, and the other players promptly fold. The aces then re-raise, and it is now two more bets to you. Do you call or fold?

5. You hold trip 7s, two of which are hidden as your hole cards. The remaining 7 is live, and only two of the cards that would pair your kickers and fill you up are dead. You're in late position. A pair of 10s has bet four dollars, and four people before you have called. Do you call or raise?

6. You're in middle position. You hold a four-straight, but you've seen three of your needed cards fall. A player with a pair of kings bets, and he's called by a three-flush. The next two players fold, and the action comes to you. When you look to see who is yet to act, you notice a small pair. Do you fold or call?

7. You have a pair and pocket aces that haven't improved. To make matters worse, you've been dealt mediocre cards on the board, and one of your aces is dead. A pair of 9s bets, and the action is to you. A player with three diamonds showing and another smaller pair has yet to act. Do you call, fold or raise?

8. You've made a powerful full house – kings full. On the board, there is a pair of 10s and a pair of deuces. Two of your kings are showing, so you are the player to start the action. Bet or check?

9. You've made a full house, but this time it's small – 4s full. A pair of aces has bet, and you are second to act. You notice that there are a pair of 10s and a pair of 6s yet to act. Do you call or raise?

10. You have completed a straight. On the board, a pair of 6s was the high hand, and its owner has bet. Two other players called, and now the action is to you. You notice a three-flush and a three-straight on the board; both are bigger than yours and are yet to act. Do you call or raise?

Answers

1. Raise. You have a good two pair here, so protect it. There is no higher pair on the board, so drive out the drawing hands and narrow the field as much as possible to reduce your competition.

2. Fold. Here the decision is very simple, and you can fold without a second thought. Sure, you may have live cards, but with a small two pair, you are going up against two bigger pairs on the board. If they have two pair or better and you don't fill up, you lose. If you do fill up, but they do as well, you still lose. So don't chase this hand – fold and be done with it.

3. Call. Calling is the best move here because you are hoping to stay in cheaply. Some people would even advise you to raise here (a semi-bluff), since you are even money to get the flush, and raising will force out other players and gain you a free card on sixth street. That's a stretch. Wait until you make your hand before raising. Certainly don't fold. With only four of your cards dead, there are still five left in the deck that can help you.

4. Fold. It may be tempting to call here, since you think of it as your money in the pot. But you can't think that way. Such heavy action here indicates that the players have made good hands. Perhaps they've even filled up, and at the least they have trips. You haven't made a straight yet, and it's not worth the money to draw to what may very well be the second best hand.

5. Raise. It's very easy to fall into the trap of wanting to be passive here – you have that good but not great hand. If you had two pair of 7s up, you'd want to fold, but with trips, even though there is a higher pair on the board, a raise is the best move. It will send a warning sign to other players. Some will stay in, but you still want to play aggressively and hope at least one will drop. Those trips and big two pairs *have to be protected.*

6. Fold. Those straight-draws can be death traps, and this is a prime example. You are looking at a big pair and a possible flush. And on top of that, three of your cards needed to improve are gone, so you should be, too. The only time you can consider calling is if you have a big pair to go with your straight draw (such as if your hand were T J Q A A).

7. Fold. Yes, it's painful – you had those beautiful pocket aces, and now you have to fold them. If you were playing hold 'em, you'd be playing them hard, but there are no community cards in stud, and your aces that once were strong are now weak. One is dead, and a pair on the board has bet. On top of that, you could be looking at a player on a good flush draw or another player who has made two pair or trips. So, fold and wait until you have a better hand down the line.

8. Check. You'd do best to play this hand slowly. It's a monster, and the odds of its being beaten are very slim. If someone bets into your open pair of cowboys, just call unless he has an ace showing. If he does, raise him. Sure, you could check-raise, but why not set a trap? You're full, and he obviously doesn't know that. Playing this hand slowly will keep other players in the game and win you a good pot.

9. Raise. Before, when you had a big full house, calling and checking until sixth street was the right move. A smaller full house is still a great hand, but it *is* beatable. It therefore needs to be protected, especially when there are bigger pairs on the board. Make the aces call your raise. The remaining players will have to call two big bets to stay in.

Many of them may fold, and your pot may not be as huge, but that's okay. Too many players make the mistake here of just calling, and few things are as frustrating as having a player turn over a larger full house than yours smile, and say, "The river was good to me." Don't let him even get to the river.

10. Raise. You can't let fear run your betting. Calling will let your opponents stay in cheaply when they are on probable draws. You want to play aggressively, making those yet to act pay two big bets to play, and making the 6s call your raise to stick around. Like trips, a straight here is quite good. Often times it's not good enough, though, so, unless there are compelling reasons not to (such as a raising war between players with two big pairs on the board), protect your hand.

6

SIXTH STREET

Play on sixth street is like stopping to fill up your car with gas on a road trip – you make a brief stop along the way to your destination. In this case, your destination is seventh street – the showdown – and you can't get there without stopping at sixth street along the way. The majority of the times you're on sixth street, you'll either be playing hard or trying to limp to the river to complete your hand.

There will, however, be a few times when you will have to lay down a hand at sixth street. Most of the time, though, you'll use sixth street to build up the pot before it is turned over to you, or to sweat it out and pray to the poker gods that the river will yield you that beautiful card to complete your hand. In this section, we'll look at the different ways you need to play at this stage of the hand.

The Monster Hands

You've been staring at those three jacks for what seems like the longest time, and you're playing your hand beautifully. But there's that knot in your stomach – you're hoping and praying to complete your full house so you can be more at ease and certain that you'll win this pot. And then, it happens. The perfect card comes to give you that monster full house or, wonder of wonders, quad jacks. Ah, the monster hand. Few things are as beautiful.

No More Slow-Playing

So, now that you have the monster hand, what do you do with it? In the section on fifth street, I pointed out that it was a good idea to slow-play this hand. Slow-playing lets the other hands stick around while you wait for them to build up a pot that you're going to win.

But slow-playing is no longer the right thing to do here. Here you should just keep raising. You have a powerful hand, and if you bang away by raising and re-raising, you won't find that too many people will fold. Remember, for most people, sixth street is just a stop on the journey to the river, and folding here is unthinkable.

As a result, no matter how much you bang away, most players are going to stay in. They feel married to their hands for having stayed in it this long. Even if a player knows he's drawing to the second-best hand, he'll pay you off anyway. Another reason so many players will stay in here no matter what you do is that the curiosity kills them. If they fold on sixth street, they will never know if they would have completed their hands or not – so it's worth it to them to call no matter what you do.

The one instance where calling with a monster hand is the best decision is if you play at a card club (as I do) where there is a "bad beat" jackpot. At my favorite card room, if you lose with aces full of 10s or better, you split a jackpot with the player you lost to, and other players at the table also get a share. If you're playing under these conditions, just check or call until the river so as not to force out players and give yourself a chance at the jackpot. If, however, you are playing in a home game or at a club that has no jackpot or a different kind of jackpot, play this hand hard – have no fear of the rest of the players folding, since that isn't going to happen. They don't care how much it costs them – they are determined to see the last card.

Quick Guide...
...to *Monster Hands* on *Sixth Street*
• **RAISE** most of the time – don't worry about slow-playing, since players are in for the long haul.
• **CALL** if you play at a card club that has a "bad beat" jackpot and your hand qualifies.

Completed Solid Hands (Straights or Better)

Considering that the average winning hand in stud poker is three 9s, a straight or better will frequently win you the pot. But depending on what else is going on at the table, different situations call for different styles of play. Most of the time, however, when you complete a hand you've been drawing to, you want to play it as hard as you can.

Suppose that you hold a flush and are in middle position. It's one bet back to you. Unless you are looking at trips on the board or a bigger four-flush yet to act, you'll be raising the stakes to build up the pot or to try to force out a player who's looking at big odds against his making his hand.

Don't try for a check-raise here – either bet or raise. Raising may not force out as many people as it would have at fifth street, but it will make them pay more to see their cards. When you have a good hand that you believe will win, that's what you want them to do – give you their chips. Playing your hand hard can occasionally force out a player or two on that very marginal draw. That's also good, since even the biggest odds are occasionally overcome.

Calling

Aggressive play is the right decision most of the time, but there are a few times when calling is the right move. One instance is if a player with very threatening cards on the board has bet. When this happens, he won't be raised all that often, since other players will be scared. If you've seen a lot of cards to complete his hand fall, a raise might be in order – if it will get you heads up against that player. This probably won't happen since, as I've said, so many players are married to their hands and will be staying in. So, if you face a bet from two pair, trips, or a bigger four-flush or four-straight than you have, unless you believe the player to be bluffing based on your knowledge of him or you've realized that many of the cards he needs are dead, just call.

Stay Unless Second-Best

In the previous chapter, in the section on drawing hands, I noted that you have to think long and hard about staying in when it's two big bets to you. Here the decision is more straightforward – you've made your hand, and you want to stick around with a flush or better until the end, *unless* you get a strong feeling that it is the second best hand. This is a sense that will come only by having a good feel and knowledge of your opponents at the table.

With a straight, you can be more cautious. You can even consider folding the hand with two big bets back to you more frequently than with the flush. Early on, I mentioned that I didn't care for straight draws. I don't even care for completed straights all that much, as they have cost me more money then I care to mention here. So, if it's two big bets to you and you hold a straight, call if you feel you have the best hand, but if you're looking at a four flush or trips on the board, fold the straight.

Another indicator that will help you decide whether or not to stay in with a completed flush will be its size – is it a big flush or a small flush? If you hold a 9-high flush, you certainly don't want to raise a four-flush on the board that could be higher than yours. As was the case on fifth street, a raise from a big bet is an indication that a player has made a very good hand – usually a flush or better. If you get this kind of indication, proceed with caution.

It's not likely that you'll face two big bets until the showdown, but if you face them on sixth street, call only if you strongly feel that you have the best hand. Of course, remembering dead cards will help you immensely. If you hold a flush and face a raise from a four-flush that is higher, but you see a lot of dead cards that would have helped your opponent, you can feel more comfortable calling.

Again, knowing your opponent is the best of all indicators when you're faced with two big bets. While bluffing is not all that common in the low limits, when it does occur, it will often be from a player who has a four-flush on the board. He'll raise, believing that everyone will figure him for the flush and fold. If you know him to be the type of player that will do that, don't hesitate to call. But always evaluate your situation carefully when you face two big bets. Ideally, you'll be the one who makes other players yet to act face two big bets to stay in to the river, but when you have to deal with them, play your hand very carefully.

Raising

Yes, that's right, there are times when raising with a hand such as a flush is the best decision, even when it's two big bets to you. For one thing, at sixth street, a bet raised by another player could be an attempt to force you out. The raiser may think that you haven't made your hand when you already have. If it looks like that's the case, go ahead and re-raise or cap the pot. Make him pay dearly for his decision. If you feel that you have the best hand, don't fear a raise – go ahead and re-raise it.

In most cases, though, calling when you face two big bets on sixth street is the correct decision when you've made a solid but not stellar hand. You should rarely lay down a completed good hand unless you have a great knowledge of your opponents or your gut tells you that you have only the second-best hand.

Here's another thing to keep in mind at sixth street that will help you determine how to bet – a player must have a pair on the board in order to have a full house. I've mentioned before that stud can be more challenging than hold 'em, since you never know when you have "the nuts." At sixth street, you can at least know when your opponent has no chance of having the boat. With a bet or even two bets but no pairs from either the bettor or the raiser, you can feel more confident in banging away with your hand – unless it looks like one of your opponents has made a bigger flush or straight.

Most of the time you'll be happy to have made a good hand at sixth street, so look for a reason not to play. Generally, sixth street is just a stopping point on your way to the showdown. Unless it looks very bleak, stick with your made flush or straight. Call if you aren't sure it's the best, and bang away with confidence when it seems that it is.

Quick Guide...
...to *Solid but not Stellar Hands* on *Sixth Street*

- **RAISE** if you feel that you have the best hand.
- **CALL** when you are not as confident about your hand, and it looks like someone else might have you beat.
- **FOLD** a flush or straight at sixth street rarely – only if you feel that your hand has become second best.

Trips and Two Pairs

In previous chapters, we discussed how you want to play trips and two pairs aggressively to force out drawing hands and make them pay dearly to stick around. This was especially the case at fifth street, when you could bet the maximum and make the drawing hands pay more to stay in the hand. Having read that last sentence, you may be thinking that this section isn't even necessary. Just follow what you learned before and it will work here, right?

Unfortunately, that's not the case. More than once in this chapter I've noted that sixth street is just a stop on your way to your final destination of seventh street. At this stage in the game, the players are either in or they're out. Raising won't force players out too often, so you should raise only when you feel you have the best hand.

When I play hold 'em, and I've made a set of aces or a big two pair on the turn (sixth) card, I'm going to be raising and banging away. Anyone who plays hold 'em knows that trips and big two pairs have to be played hard. Many players enjoy both hold 'em and stud, but you can't get them confused. Trips and two pairs in stud are not nearly as valuable as trips and sets in hold 'em.

In stud, you just want to call with these hands. The only reason you would want to raise is if it seems that the other players are very weak and they're just trying to limp to the river as cheaply as possible. For example, let's say you have three kings and two players remain. Both check to you and show nothing on the board. Here, you could go ahead and bet – you'll win extra money, since they are going to stay in anyway if they have stayed this far into the hand.

Rarely Lay Down That Hand

When we discussed flushes and straights, I mentioned that you need to look for a reason not to play the hand until the end. This is true with trips and two pairs as well – unless there is some compelling reason not to, play them until the end and hope they will either win you the pot alone or improve. Four considerations will contribute to your decision to fold two pairs or trips at sixth street:

1) The knowledge you have of your opponent
2) How serious the board looks
3) How many of your cards and your opponents' cards are live
4) Which your hand is – trips or two pair

While most of the time you won't be folding, there are times when the decision is not that hard. For instance, let's say you have two pair – jacks and 7s. A jack and a 7 are dead already, which leaves two cards that can help you. A player with a pair of queens on the board bets, and he is raised by a four-flush.

Here, it's clearly not the best move to stay in. Sure, there are two cards in the deck that could give you a full house, but you are already an underdog to make the hand, and you are a huge underdog to win the pot. You could be looking at a flush and either trip queens or queens full, which would beat your jacks full even if you make the hand.

Of course, another factor that will help you determine whether to stay or to fold will be what you hold – is it two pair or trips? I'd rather be holding trips at this point in the hand. Calling two big bets can be justified with trips, but some warning bells had better go off in your head when you are faced with two big bets while holding two pair.

The reason is in the odds. When you have trips with one card left, your odds against getting your full house are 4 to 1. With two pair, however, they are *10* to 1. Not good. In either situation, if you do stay in, you'll want to have live cards – but the decision to call two big bets is much more justifiable with trips than with two pair.

Even if you are 4 to 1 against making a full house with trips, you're probably getting good pot odds for your bet. Two big bets in a $2/4 game would be eight dollars, and at this point the pot would probably have at least $32 in it. Since you're probably getting better than 4 to 1 pot odds on your bet, calling is clearly best, unless, of course, you are calling a bet raised by something that looks very dangerous, such as open trips on the board which are higher than your trips. Even though you don't want to fold at sixth street, you should generally do so with two pair when you're faced with two big bets – unless you really want to spend that money to chase one card that will help you when you are probably already beaten.

In my experience, facing two big bets on sixth street hasn't been that common. It's much more common to face two big bets on the showdown at seventh street. However, it still does happen occasionally on sixth street, so when you do face such a situation, you must determine whether to play when it will cost you a lot of chips to do so. Stay in only when it looks like you can improve your hand and when you are getting the right kind of pot odds. Putting it simply, with two big bets, you'd better have trips that aren't dwarfed by a bigger set of trips.

Folding

Should you ever fold your trips or two pair when it's just one bet to stay in? Generally not, unless it looks like you'll be beat. Look back at the example of trips on the board. Rarely will someone raise trips that are open for everyone to see, so folding against them when you have a smaller set or two pair is certainly a wise decision. So, too, is folding when you have too many dead cards to justify going on to the river and the board looks too tough. Let's say you have 10s and 6s. Not too bad, but not too good either. A 10 and a 6 are dead, a pair of aces bets, and now it's to you. Unless you've noticed that the other aces are dead, fold.

Quick Guide...

...to *Trips & Two Pairs* on *Sixth Street*

- **RAISE** rarely. You can't be feeling too certain about this hand, unless it looks like the other players are so weak and loose that they've been staying in for no reason.
- **CALL** most of the time – you've stayed this far with your hand, so, if you can, stay to the end.
- **FOLD** when you feel you will be beat.

Pairs

You shouldn't have played your pair past fifth street unless you were either getting cards for free or had possibilities for other hands, such as a flush or straight. If your situation hasn't improved here on sixth street and you're still looking at a pair, don't play unless you have four-to-a-straight or four-to-a-flush to go with your pair. If that is the case, you'll want to stick around to the end. Your odds to get the flush are about 4 to 1, and your odds to get the straight are about 5 to 1. You also have other outs, since you could improve to trips or a solid two pair. A four-dollar bet is going into a pot large enough to justify your calling.

Again, as with other hands, strongly consider folding if you have to call two big bets. You are certainly in the weakest position here with just a pair – you could very well be drawing dead to a hand that will be bigger than your straight or flush if you should hit it. While calling two big bets with a flush already made is much more justifiable, calling here isn't – you'll only hit that flush one out of every four times. Unless that pot is enormous, fold.

Of course, don't give any consideration to playing to seventh street with a pair that hasn't improved to a four-straight or a four-flush. If you stayed past fifth street with a pair because you were hoping to catch two running cards if your pair didn't improve, and you didn't get any help, muck the hand. Most of the time you wouldn't have been playing this hand anyway, unless you had a lot of live cards. Even if you did, it's certainly not worth staying in the hand with a pair that has no chance to improve to a flush or straight – the most you'll have in the end is trips.

> ## Quick Guide...
> ### ...to *Pairs* on *Sixth Street*
> • **CALL** if you have a four-flush or four-straight to go with your pair.
> • **FOLD** if you were on a three-straight or three-flush with your pair at fifth street that didn't improve here at sixth street.

Drawing Hands

Once you've stayed in the hand this long, you will want to look for a compelling reason not to continue and see this hand until the end. These reasons rarely arise.

The only time you want to consider laying down your drawing hand (four-to-a-flush or four-to-a-straight) is when you get the strong feeling that you are drawing dead – if, for example, you held four-to-a-flush or four-to-a-straight, and you began to see a lot of heavy action on the board from hands that looked more powerful.

For instance, let's say you hold 9 10 J Q, and your straight draw is live. Before the betting gets to you, a four-flush bets, and the bettor is re-raised by a pair of queens. You're facing two big bets, so you need to fold this hand, since you are drawing dead to possibly two hands.

You can also base your decision whether to proceed on the

status of your opponent's live cards and your knowledge of your opponent. If your opponent holds trip 6s, you have four-to-a-flush or good straight, and the action comes to you and no one has raised, you can go ahead and stay in if you have seen two of his cards fall. Studying your opponent's playing style will also pay off. You can go ahead and stick around if you know him to be the type of player who likes to try to scare people off. You can fold if you know him to be the type of player who plays hard only when he has made a solid hand.

Sixth Street: A Summary

In this chapter, I've pointed out that sixth street should be just a stopping point for you as you proceed on to seventh street. If you find yourself staying in a lot to see sixth street and laying down a lot of hands, take the time to review your play. Odds are that you shouldn't have been playing the hand past fifth street, and laying it down there would have saved you a lot of money. Or you might be too passive, and you're laying down decent hands, with which you should have stayed in to see the last card.

Even though *most* of the time you'll be staying to see the last card, you certainly won't be doing so *all* of the time. There will be situations that come up when folding at sixth street will be the right thing to do, as I've showed you. One is holding the drawing or decent (but not great) hand and looking at two bets. Evaluate your hand carefully whenever you're faced with two big bets, and stay in only if you feel confident that you hold the best hand or that if you get the card you need, you will hold the best hand.

Finally, as is always the case in poker, when you feel that you have the best hand, play it hard. Because most of the players at this stage are staying until the end, go ahead and bang away when you believe that yours is the best. Most of the time, you should be coming away with a good pot at the end.

At the same time, don't worry about not raising if you aren't sure about your hand's strength. While some of the more good but not great hands (such as trips) needed to be protected on previous rounds, raising at this stage in the hand won't drive out your opponents that often. So bang away only when you feel you have the best hand, and call when you aren't certain.

Quick Quiz: Sixth Street

Take the quick quiz below, and then let's move on to the last stage of the hand. Here all that work you've done – studying your opponents, keeping in mind live cards, and remembering the odds – will pay off.

Questions

1. You hold four to a flush and are in late position. Five of the cards you'd need to improve are gone, leaving you with four left in the deck to help you. On the board, a pair of 9s has bet, and a pair of 5s has called. There have been several other callers, including what looks to be a possible straight and a possible flush that, if made, appears to be lower than yours. Do you call or fold?

2. You hold two pair – 7s and 4s. Both of your 7s are gone.

A pair of aces on the board has bet, and the bettor has been raised by a four-flush which seems to have live cards. You're third to act; do you call or fold?

3. You have trip 9s, two of which are showing. The other 9 is alive, and, looking at your three kickers, you notice that three cards that would fill you up are gone. In middle position, a pair of 7s bet, and the better was followed by two callers, one with a pair of 5s and another with a four-straight. Do you call or raise?

4. You have four to an inside straight draw. One of the cards that would complete your hand is dead. A pair of kings bet, and the bet was called by both a four-flush and a pair of 6s. Do you call or fold?

5. You've made a flush. A pair of 9s bet, and the bettor was raised by a possible straight showing on the board. There were two callers: a player with a pair of 5s and a player with three suited cards on the board. Do you call or raise?

6. You hold a pair of queens on the board in middle position. You stayed in on fifth street because you had a three-flush, but you got no help here. A pair of kings bet and received two callers who look to be on straight and flush draws respectively. Nothing too threatening will follow behind you. Your kickers include an ace and jack, of which just one is dead. Your queens are also live. Do you call or fold?

7. You hold four to an open-ended straight, and two of the cards you need to complete your straight are dead. On the board, two pair – queens and 7s – was high and bet. You're in middle position, and the other players folded, making it one bet to you. Do you call or fold?

8. You have a solid two pair – aces and 9s. One ace is dead, but the rest of your cards are live. You're in early position, and a pair of jacks bet first. Two players are yet to act: one whom you feel is on a flush draw (he has three-to-a-flush showing), and one with a pair of 5s. As the second person to act, do you raise or call?

9. You have made a good full house, jacks full. The board looks weak. You are first to act and have a pair of jacks showing. Do you check or bet?

10. You have trip 5s and are in late position. Unfortunately for you, there are trip 7s on the board. The holder of the 7s bets, and he is raised by a pair of aces. The rest of the players fold, and it's to you. Your cards are mostly live. Do you call the two big bets or fold?

Answers

1. Call. Remember, sixth street is just a brief stop on the way to seventh. You may have five dead cards, but you've been in it this far. Stay to the end and hope to complete your hand.

2. Fold. You won't be doing much folding on sixth street, but here the reasons to fold are clear. Your two pair is mediocre, you have two dead cards, and you are looking at what could be trip aces or better and a possible flush. The odds don't justify staying in here, so fold the hand.

3. Raise. Trips will win many pots, and you want to protect the hand. If the possible straight had raised, it would have been best to call, but a call from him means he's probably on a draw. Make him pay, and drive out others with your raise. Many times you will call with trips, since most people will stay in on sixth street. But a raise can be justified if you believe you have the best hand.

4. Fold. You could make the case to call if you had a quality straight draw or a good pair with the four-straight, but here it's best to fold. The odds are a whopping 10.5 to 1 to get your straight – facing those kinds of odds, be done with the hand. If you had an open-ended straight you certainly could stay in, but not on an inside-straight draw.

5. Raise. You want to play this hand aggressively. Don't let a flush draw stay in cheaply, and drive out those other players. This hand is very solid, but it's not a monster, and it therefore needs to be played hard.

6. Fold. If you said, "call," your answer is understandable – you have a lot of possible outs here. But if I'm holding just one pair here and I'm already beaten, I fold. The kings very well may have two pair, so even if you make two pair on the river you have a good chance of losing. Trips would also lose to the straight or flush draws if they complete their hands. It stinks to fold on sixth street, but doing so is the right decision here.

7. Call. If you can pick up a tell that would indicate that the player has made a full house, fold. A fold would also be okay if all of his cards were live. Most of the time, though, once you've stayed in this far, you want to call if it is just one bet. Bluffing doesn't work too often at the low limits, but that won't stop players from trying to bluff. Watch your opponent carefully as he gets his river card, and try to get clues as to whether he has made his hand.

8. Call. Two pair will frequently win, especially when it's a good two pair like aces up. Raise to protect it on fifth street, but call with it here, since you won't get players to drop out.

9. Bet. At fifth street, you could have slow-played this hand. Now, though, most players will stay in. Many will be focused on trying to make their hands, which, if they do, will be second best to yours. Go ahead and bet – they'll stick around.

10. Fold. Think about it this way: the player with the trip 7s was first to act, and he was raised. Few people are stupid enough to raise trips on the board unless they have something big themselves. Trips for you are *usually* a great hand and you *usually* have to play hard to protect them. But if there are circumstances that present themselves that indicate you don't have the best hand, just fold – even if it hurts.

7

SEVENTH STREET

Ah, seventh street. You've mucked so many hands on third, had so many that had promise early on but had to be folded at fifth, and, for what seems like an eternity, have been on the sidelines watching the dealer push the chips to the other players. But, now you're here.

Hopefully you're here because you have been playing smart, so you now have a good hand that you are confident will be the winner. At this point, you won't have to worry about remembering cards anymore – there are no more to come. On seventh street, you either have the hand or you don't, and hopefully you do. If you didn't make the hand, the decision is easy – fold. But if you have made the hand, determining whether to raise or to call is challenging. This section will help you understand that decision-making process.

In each of the previous chapters and sections, we've analyzed the different types of hands, starting with the best ones and ending with the less desirable ones. I've then summarized each section to help you keep in mind what to take with you when you go to the card club or when you are reviewing this book. This section will be laid out a little differently. Rather than analyzing each hand, I've made this chapter a "big summary" of sorts, so the focus will be on the situations in which you should raise, the situations in which you should call, and finally the situations in which laying down your hand is best.

I've constructed this chapter differently because seventh street is unique – here you'll see a lot of action from players, and there are no more cards to come. In earlier rounds, your goal was to defend hands and drive out opponents. You'll certainly be happy when a player folds after you've bet or raised on seventh street, but your focus here is on winning the biggest possible pot when you have a great hand, and on winning a small or medium pot with a hand that is more marginal. No matter what you hold though, you'll have to know when you can raise, call, and fold. First on tap is the best situation – when you want to raise.

Raising on Seventh Street

When you've made a monster hand – such as quads, a straight flush, or a big full house – raising is pretty much a no-brainer. With these hands, there is very little doubt that you'll win the pot, so you'll want to be raising and re-raising as much as possible. If it's a bet to you, raise and re-raise until the pot is capped. With your huge hand, if your opponents don't lay down their hands, they'll be paying you off.

Unless there are compelling reasons not to raise (such as open trips on the board representing a potential boat higher than yours), raise with a full house. With a boat, you have a wonderful hand that will win the pot the vast majority of the time, so whenever it's one bet to you, you should be looking for a reason to not raise. A call is okay if you are not too certain about the strength of your hand, but as long as you feel comfortable, raise. Not doing so will take away from what could have been a bigger pot. If you are naturally conservative and tight, as I tend to be, this can be tough – we all remember those good hands that didn't hold up, and we don't want to go down that road again if we don't have to.

A full house is a powerful hand, though, which is why you want to raise unless something looks ominous. The obvious ominous situation would be if you were holding a small or medium-sized full house and a player had trips on the board that could represent a bigger full house than yours. In that case, it would be an easy decision to call.

Another situation in which you'd call would be when there were two pair on the board that, if full, would be higher than your boat – and the two cards that would make the hand a full house higher than yours were live. If only one card were live in that situation, you could go ahead and either bet or raise – two pair may be all your opponent has, and there is just one card in the deck that will help him out. If he re-raises, though, just call.

As I've emphasized time and time again, whenever you feel that you have the best hand, go ahead and raise. Let's say you had a four-flush on sixth street and called, and now you've made a good flush. It's one bet to you, and you don't see anything that looks too threatening from either the player who bet or those yet to act. With a flush, you have a very solid hand, so raise. You'd call only if you felt that the player who bet had a full house, or if you were facing two big bets.

Don't Turn Into a Calling Station

Before we look at the right situations in which to call, something to keep in mind is that you should not find yourself turning into a calling station on seventh street. Many players make this mistake. It doesn't matter if they have an ace-high flush or a full house – unless they have a monster hand such as quads, they won't raise. You should not be one of these people. Obviously, it's easy to fall into this trap. You're so happy to win the pot that you miss the chance to maximize your winnings. By playing a solid hand more aggressively, you can win even more money.

That's why it's important to be aggressive when you do have a great hand – bang away. There may be a time or two when you read an opponent wrong, or when your 8s full gets beat by 9s full – every poker player remembers those times. But to go along with those are the times when you will win a big pot, and those will outweigh the times you lose a big pot. Make the most of those circumstances by playing your hand hard whenever you think it's the best.

Most of the time this will be when you have made a full house, but even with a strong flush, if you think it's the best, go with that instinct. You'll be sitting out a lot of hands in stud poker, so you want to maximize your opportunities whenever you have the chance.

Calling on Seventh Street

The factors that determine when to call on seventh street are very similar to the factors you considered at sixth street. Many times, you'll have a hand such as trips or a straight – it isn't bad, but neither is it stellar. You don't want to fold such a hand, since odds are it very well might win you the pot. At the same time, reaching for chips to bet makes you anxious, because you worry that you just might be betting into a bigger hand than what you hold.

Don't Hesitate to Stick Around

Once you've played your hand this far, if you hold a good two pair and there is no higher pair or better on the board, stay in for at least one bet. In this situation, you must look for a reason that tells you to fold. If you can't find one, stick around. On the showdown, a player might turn over a straight or trips and beat you, but it was worth it to see that hand, since you held a good hand as well. There are some situations when you should lay down this hand, but when you have a good hand, calling at least one bet is the best move. Many times a big two pair will win you the pot, so stay in unless warning signs present themselves.

Calling on seventh street can be summed up with five words: *go with your gut feeling*. When you like but don't love your hand, call if it looks like there could be threatening hands yet to act, or if you know your opponent to bluff rarely and play only the solid hands. On the show-down, you may find that your hand was the best one and breathe a big sigh of relief. Don't feel bad about having called, not raised – you made the right decision, since you did not feel too confident about your hand. While you shouldn't turn into a calling station on the river, calling is always the best move when you feel uncertain about the strength of your hand.

Don't be the Table Sheriff

Before we move on, one more piece of advice: don't turn into the poker sheriff. Identifying a player who wants to be one is easy – he will use the phrase, "Well, I'll call to keep you honest." You shouldn't be calling unless you have a decent hand. Your job is to win the pot, not to be the sheriff of the table. Remember, you don't encounter much bluffing at the low limits. The only time that you can call a player who has bet when you think you're beat is if you know him very, very well – so when you feel you are beat, fold the hand and don't throw money away.

Folding on Seventh Street

Nobody likes to fold, and once you've invested this much into a hand, folding is especially undesirable. Most of the time, when you have a hand of some sort, you will be staying in. Still, there are those dreaded times when you do have to fold your hand.

First and most obvious is when you do not make your hand. You had a flush draw with lots of live cards in your suit, and that last diamond didn't fall. Here, you obviously want to fold the hand. The only possible time when you could play a busted flush or straight is when you have four to the flush or straight on the board. Still, playing that hand is not really a good idea. At the low limits, even with something as scary as a four-flush on the board, it's rare that all the players left in the pot will be spooked by a possible flush or straight and fold. The vast majority of the time, at least someone will stay in the pot to "keep you honest," and you'll have been throwing money away.

Be Wary of Raising Wars

Folding is also the right course of action when you have that good but not great hand and are up against a raising war. These are the low limits, not $30/60 stud, but raising wars still do break out, and when they do, they are most likely to be on seventh street. If you are in one, and you feel confident about your hand, bang away. But when one breaks out and you are not sure about the strength of your hand, don't feel bad about folding.

Whenever a raising war breaks out, it means two players have made very good hands and they feel confident enough to invest a lot of money. Your trips or small straight simply isn't going to hold up – so just muck the hand. And, yes, that does include when you've already put money into the pot. Let's look at an example.

Say you hold trip jacks and are first to act. Believing you have the best hand, you bet. Another player raises your bet – he has a pair of queens on the board – and a four-flush promptly re-raises him. Some players can't resist calling two additional big bets because they have already put some of their money in the pot – but the player who does that *must not be you.*

Even with money in the pot on this round, when a raising war breaks out or when you face two big bets, the best move is to fold any hand that's less than a flush. It's not likely to hold up, because a raise here indicates *strength.* When you have a strong straight, it's okay to call two bets *only* if it looks like the bettor and raiser don't have a flush or better. If they do, just fold. Also fold your flush when faced with two big bets if you feel you are going up against a full house or bigger flush. After all, the second-best hand in poker wins you nothing.

In conclusion, you will be calling or raising much more often than you will be folding on seventh street. Even so, you will have to fold from time to time on the river – especially when you don't make your hand. Don't try to be the poker police and think you'll call someone's bluff – remember, bluffing is a rarity at the low limits.

Also, don't go against your instincts when they are telling you your hand won't hold up. Calling one bet with a straight or flush is fine – with two bets to you or when in the midst of a raising war, unless you have a good quality flush, don't feel bad about folding the hand. One of the players will have what he is representing – a hand that's bigger than yours.

Quick Quiz: Seventh Street

Questions

1. You hold two pair – queens and 4s – and are in middle position. A player with a pair of 9s is first to act, and he bets. Several other players call; one holds a three-flush, and another holds a pair of 6s. The bet is to you. Do you fold or call?

2. You've made your flush, and it's of good quality – queen-high. You're in late position. A pair of kings bet first, and the bettor was raised by a four-flush with a jack-high. There were two callers, and the rest of the players folded. The only player who will act after you has nothing showing that poses a threat. Do you call or raise?

3. You have four-to-a-flush on the board, but you didn't make your hand. The board looks weak, and players have received many free cards. The pot is relatively small, and a pair of 7s is the high hand on the board. That player bets. You're in late position, and the next few players fold. By the time it gets to you, you would be the third person in the pot. You believe that if you raised, the last person to act would fold. Do you raise here and try a bluff or fold the hand?

4. You hold a 10-high straight and are second to act behind a pair of queens. The holder of the queens bets. Among the hands yet to act, you notice a pair of 9s and a four-flush. You call and are promptly raised by the holder of the four-flush, who is re-raised by the player with the 9s. The remaining players fold, and the player with the queens calls both raises. Do you call and hope your hand will hold up?

5. You have a four-straight on the board – T J Q K. Since there are no pairs held by any player on the board, and you have the high card, you are the first to act. You didn't make your straight on the river. Action has been relatively light thus far, and you consider betting and hoping that everyone else will fold. Should you bet or just check?

6. You have been able to limp to seventh street with a small two pair – 5s and treys. A player with a pair of 4s on the board bets, and he has three callers before the betting gets to you. Of the hands yet to act, the most threatening is a three-flush; all of the other players appear weak. Do you call or fold?

7. You have a powerful hand – aces full. A pair of your aces is on the board, and you start the betting. Do you bet or just check and hope to try a check-raise?

8. You have two pair – kings and 9s – and are last to act. There is a four-flush on the board, whose owner is second to act, and he bets after being checked to. There is one caller showing a pair of 6s, and the betting is to you. You have been keeping track of the first player's cards, and while you don't have an exact count, you believe you have seen many of his needed suit fall already. Do you call or fold?

9. Carefully watching a player who you place on a flush

draw (he has three of his suit showing on the board) you notice a slight sigh as he looks at his cards before he quickly looks up. In your hand, you hold two pair – jacks and 9s. The player with the three-flush also has a pair on the board – 4s – and his happens to be the high hand showing. He bets, and there are two callers by the time the action gets to you.

You feel confident that you have these other players beat – they show nothing threatening – and you contemplate whether to call or fold. What's the best move?

10. You have a full house – 10s full of 4s – that's completely hidden. A player with a pair of aces on the board opens, and he's raised by a four-flush. You know at least one of the other aces is dead. You are third to act, and it's two big bets to you – do you re-raise?

Answers

1. Call. This hand is almost a crapshoot, but you should play it. You've made it this far, and there hasn't been a lot of heavy betting action, so staying in to the end is the best decision. It's only one more bet, and a solid two pair can often hold up. If, however, the three-flush or pair of 6s had raised, you'd want to fold unless you know that your opponent is someone who will bluff from time to time.

2. Raise. If you've been paying attention, you can do so with even more ease, since you'll know if the bettor's other two kings are live or dead. If it is re-raised, just call. Remember, though, a flush is a very good hand, especially when it is a quality flush like the one you have. Don't worry about raising here unless you have a strong feeling another player has made a full house.

3. It depends. Bluffing rarely works at the low limits, but there are exceptions to every rule. Folding here is generally the best move. At the same time, bluffing is also not a horrible move, especially if you've been keeping track of the cards of your suit and most are live. Many players may not have even noticed, but if they *have* been paying attention to what you need to get your flush and they've noticed that most of the cards of your suit are live, a raise here just might work – especially if you've been playing for a while and have an image as a tight but aggressive player.

If you're called for your bluff, players will still have a hard time figuring out what you hold down the line, and they may very well call more hands against you when you do have them beaten. That said, don't raise and try to bluff with this hand *all* the time – it's the most common bluff attempt in low-limit stud, and more times than not, at least one player will call you, so if you fold every time you don't complete a flush with four-to-the-flush on the board, you're playing good, solid poker.

4. Fold. You've been with your hand a long time, have some money invested in the pot, and would like to call, but you can't in this situation. You have a good hand, but unfortunately for you, it won't hold up here. A player with a four-flush wouldn't raise with two pairs on the board unless he really liked to bluff – which isn't likely here at the low limits. Facing two big bets like this, you're best just to fold your hand.

5. Check. Attempting a bluff here would not be a total blunder, but it's still not the best move. Remember, a player doesn't have to have any pair showing on seventh street to have a full house. Even if he had just two suited cards on the board, he could also have made a flush. If you were the very last person to act and everyone had checked to you, a bluff attempt would be more justifiable – especially with four big cards such as you have on the board. In this situation, just check or fold.

6. Fold. Often a good two pair can win a pot, but the key word there is "good." Here, if you were last to act and there was just the original bettor, you could have stayed in – he was showing a pair smaller than your two pair. But with three callers, odds are that somebody has something better than 5s over treys. A call isn't worth it here, so just fold.

7. Bet. It's okay to try a check-raise sometimes, but only if you have a full house or other monster hand completely hidden. Checking with a pair of aces will send warning signs to other players that you are trying to check-raise them, so go ahead and bet. You should get a lot of callers anyway, since most people, having been in the hand this long, will want to see it to the end.

8. Call. This is the classic bluff attempt (mentioned in Question #3) by the player who tries to use four-to-a-flush to scare other players off and win himself a nice pot. With four of his suit on the board, odds are he very well may have the flush. But if you feel that many of his needed cards are dead (five or more) calling is the best move. If he has the flush, it's not the end of the world – just four dollars. It was worth playing with a good quality two pair.

9. Call. This one is pretty obvious. Here, carefully watching your opponents will pay off. If you feel you have the other players beat (that your opponent was on a flush draw and didn't make a flush or trips), go ahead and call him. Tells are difficult and take a long time to learn, but seventh street is a good spot to start learning them.

10. Re-raise. You have to take advantage of powerful hands when you have them. You could be going up against a full house bigger than yours, but the raise didn't come from the holder of the aces; it came from the holder of the four-flush, who's trying to force the aces to fold.

If it were the other way around, and the player with the four-flush had bet and was raised by the player with the pair of aces, a call would be more justifiable. Of course, a bad beat here is not out of the question – full houses do occasionally lose – but with a relatively big boat like 10s full, you should play it hard. If the holder of the aces re-raises, though, all you can do is call.

8

FINAL THOUGHTS

We've now covered proper play of hands through each of the betting stages. If you read this material (and re-read it) you can head to the card club or your favorite home game with confidence, knowing when to sit tight and when to come out like a 500-pound gorilla. Before we finish up, I'd also like to mention a few last topics to help you improve your stud poker game.

Online Play

Lately it seems like millions of websites are added to the World Wide Web everyday. With the Web's incredible growth, a number of opportunities for gambling on the Internet – playing the slots, betting on sports, and, of course, playing poker – have developed. Should you play online?

Personally, I play on the Internet only for fun. I don't feel that there is anything wrong with playing online, but I prefer holding the cards in my hands, watching my opponents, and actually picking up chips. One problem with playing on the Internet is that collusion is easy there. I saw just how easy it is when I tried it with another poker player one evening. We went to a poker website to play for fun, but we let each other know what we were holding. I'm certainly not the kind of person who would ever do this in a live money game on the Web, but we did it as an experiment to determine how it would work.

The obvious result was that we both would win a number of play chips – when one of us had a monster hand, we would both drive up the pot to pay that person off. This kind of collusion was quite simple – we just communicated via instant messaging, and no one at the table knew. Doing this at a real money table would be highly unethical, but people do – so if you do play online that's one thing you need to keep in mind.

I understand that online play has become very popular, so I do not want to paint a bleak and dark picture and suggest that playing on the Internet is entirely a bad proposition. Most of the sites out there have good security, and their teams try to track down people who collude to make sure they do not disrupt play. Still, tracking down these cheaters is much more difficult on the Internet than in an actual card club. So how do you avoid them?

Well, it's definitely better to play the low limits. At the low limits that this book covers, collusion is less likely than at the higher limits. Most of the players are at those sites just for fun or to win a little money. If you are the type of player who'd collude, why would you waste your time in a low-limit online game when you could make real money cheating a higher limit game?

FINAL THOUGHTS

Pros of Online Play

Online play also has a number of advantages, especially for the low limit stud player. The biggest is that it's much easier to remember cards when you're on the computer and at home. You can have a digital notebook open, or you can use a pencil and paper to write down cards as they are folded. And that's much easier than trying to remember them all at a card club table. Additionally, if you want to, you can play in several games at once, you don't have to worry about attire, and the rake is a little lower overall.

You also have greater options in table choices (especially for us low-limit players). Some online poker sites even have tables where the minimum bet is a quarter and the big bet is fifty cents. Your take certainly won't be much from these games, but you can still learn a bit and have some fun. Online sites also have numerous play money tables, which are great when you can't get to the card club. When you do play online at a play money table, remember that the style of play will be much more loose – after all, if it's just fake money, why not gamble more?

Finally, in many states, poker is still illegal. If you are unfortunate enough to live in one of these places, here's my advice: move. If that is not an option, online poker may be your only option outside of home games with your friends. You may have to stick to playing on the Internet if you can't get to a card room.

One thing is for certain – the Internet will only grow in terms of the options you have in playing poker there.

Competition is always good, as it brings out the best in competitors to offer the best for the customer. While collusion may always be a threat, don't feel uncomfortable about playing on the Internet. For many people, Internet poker can be fun and relaxing in the comfort of their own homes.

Check-Raising

One thing that I haven't covered in depth is check-raising. First, if anyone says that it's unethical to check-raise, tell him to stick the game in his kitchen. Check-raising is a part of poker, and it's a very useful thing to do when it's done right. The key is knowing when it is right to attempt a check-raise.

Though theoretically you can check-raise at any time, the earlier your position, the better. Obviously, for you to check, there must be no bets on the table, so usually when you check-raise you will be first to act. If you are going to try for a check-raise, you want to have a monster hand or feel very confident that no one at the table has something that could beat you. Check-raising with two pair on fifth street, for instance, is not a good idea. Check-raising on fifth street with a big full house is. Even if no one bets, you get all those drawing hands in on sixth street when you'll be betting.

Having a monster hand does not automatically mean that you should check-raise. For one thing, you'll also want to be certain that another player will bet. If you have trips on the board and you check, don't expect a whole lot of callers. Hidden power is better. If your cards on the board don't reveal much, and it looks like another player could have made a hand smaller than yours or will be betting with a pair he has showing, check and then raise him and the other callers.

Don't feel guilty about check raising – it's a part of poker. Just remember that you must have a huge hand and be confident that others will bet when you try it. Check-raising with either smaller hands or with an obvious monster hand can be costly.

Keep Records

Another thing you'll want to be sure to do when you play any type of poker is keep records. It's not that hard. For a very basic poker record, just write down the date, length of time you played, and how much you won or lost. This will help you if you happen to win a lot for tax purposes, but it will also give you an idea of how you are doing overall.

If you find yourself losing several sessions in a row, don't get too worried – everyone "runs bad" from time to time. But if you find yourself consistently losing more than you win over a long period of time, evaluate your play. Try to focus on what part of your game needs work and what can make you a better player.

Always Be Learning

If you want to become a consistent, winning card player, it's a good idea to be learning more about poker constantly. You'll be learning at the card table, but there are also plenty of ways to be learning outside of the card room. Take advantage of those opportunities. Buy more books or magazines on poker and learn new techniques. Use the Internet. Just as there are many places in which you can play poker online, there are also many places where you can learn about poker.

One of my favorite sites is www.pokerpages.com. This is an outstanding website that was recently re-designed, and it now includes places where beginners can post questions, along with message boards for finding home games and asking general or advanced questions as well.

Another site I frequent is a newsgroup that's probably the most well known on the web for poker: rec.gambling.poker. You can find this using a simple search under "groups" at www.google.com. Here you will find all sorts of posts on various poker topics, including many from people asking for others' thoughts on the proper play of different hands. You can also consider starting your own web page on poker, as I have done.

Software: A Good Investment

Computer software is very useful. It's a powerful tool that will help you a lot in your game. While play money tables at poker websites are free, you won't learn a whole lot from them, as the style of play there is incredibly loose. If you purchase software for your computer, though, you can have different opponent styles, set the table limits, and get results that are much more real-life-like.

FINAL THOUGHTS

Computer software also gives you all the statistics you could ever want, from the tightness of the game to analysis of your own play (my favorite). If you want, the software can also give you advice as to how to play each hand. Be sure to check out programs such as Wilson's *Turbo Seven-Card Stud* to help you in your game. This is a fine program. It will help you a lot in your game, and it's well worth the investment. Other companies offer similar software as well.

Table Image, Etiquette & Attitude

I've included this section particularly for those players who have never been to a card room before – it's a way to keep in mind the things that they should avoid.

Cell Phones

It seems that at every table where I play, someone is trying to talk on the phone while playing cards. I recall one instance where it got so bad the dealer had to say something to a guy. Naturally, you may be busy or need your phone for emergencies – but at the table, your focus should be on the game and not on talking on your cell. It's also rude to other players who are trying to focus on the game.

Alcohol

Avoid drinking! Having a beer is all well and fine, but that's what the bar is for. Everyone knows that as you drink more, your judgment will become more clouded. You want to be as sharp as you can, so avoid alcohol when you're playing. By the same token, if you ever see someone who obviously has been drinking, he might as well have a flashing neon sign above him saying, "Free money here." He won't be focusing on the game very well, so he should be an easy target for you.

Attire

As for table image, pretty much anything goes in a public card room. You can't be fooled by someone's style of dress – the only way you'll really be able to figure out how a player will play will be by watching him carefully and learning from his playing style. Still, you can pick up on some things, such as how he presents himself. If he has chips in no particular order in front of him and doesn't watch the play of the game carefully when he is not in the hand, it's a sign that he is more of a loose player. However, if he has chips neatly stacked and looks very focused on the game, he is tighter and a more solid player.

How should you present yourself? Wear whatever you feel comfortable playing in. Me, I always wear the same thing – a black shirt and a tie with a deck of cards or images of dogs playing poker on it. That's just what I feel comfortable playing in. Most poker players are superstitious, so if you have a favorite shirt or rabbit's foot that you feel will help you in your game, go ahead and wear it or bring it.

You want to portray yourself to the table as a tight, focused card player who is ready to play – so don't be the guy with the chips all over the place, on the phone, or watching the TV. Have your chips stacked neatly in front of you in stacks of five, ten or twenty, and be focused on the game.

FINAL THOUGHTS

Attitude

The right attitude is also fundamental to being a winning poker player. You want always to be in the proper mindset when you are playing cards. As I said early on, if you feel yourself going on tilt or starting to chase a lot of cards, get up and take a walk or cash in the rest of your chips – you won't be playing your "A" game.

Always try to remain optimistic, too, even if it has been a long time since you've been able to play a hand. The good hands will come, and when they do, you want to be focused, so you know how to play them right. If you think you're a bad player, then you'll probably go home right through the exit – without stopping off at the cashier's cage first.

A Word on Tells

When it comes to tells, there's no better source of information than Mike Caro, the "mad genius of poker," who is an expert on the subject. While I do not claim to be as much of an expert on tells as Mr. Caro, there are some tells I have noticed that are common in players at the low limits and in home games. They are most likely to occur on seventh street, but they can also happen during the earlier rounds of the hand.

One tell that players frequently exhibit occurs when they miss a hand after getting their last card. When a player gets his last card, and he hasn't made his hand, he may sigh a bit, or shake his head slightly. Some players will even pick up their three hole cards, shuffle them, slowly look at them, then frown slightly. This is a great indicator that a player did not make his hand, but it doesn't last long. For this reason, it is important to watch players' faces on seventh street. Notice how they react to their cards. That sigh or frown won't last forever, so watch your opponent to catch it. Your last card isn't going anywhere. Before you look at it, watch your opponents' faces to help clue you in as to whether they have made their hands.

Another tell is a player's showing his hand to the player next to him. Some players are blatant – they'll tap the player next to them on the shoulder and even say, "Can you believe that?!" Others are subtler. They'll shake their heads slightly and let their hands out enough so their opponents can see them.

Run from the Shaking Hand

Sure, there is that frown or sigh when a player misses his hand, but how can you tell when he has made it? One of the most common tells that gives away a powerful hand is when a player's hand shakes. A player looks down to see five beautiful diamonds, or maybe that card that turned his two pair into a full house, and when he bets, his hand begins to shake. I know, because it's something that has happened to me in the past.

This is why you not only have to look at your opponents' faces, you also have to watch their hands as they place bets. Whenever you see a player's hand shake as he is about to toss his chips in front of him to bet or raise, you'd better have a monster hand, too – because he certainly does.

FINAL THOUGHTS

Another indicator that a player has made his hand is when he looks at it very briefly. When a player is looking at his hand for a long time, either he hasn't made anything and is hoping the cards will somehow magically change, or he has made a straight and is trying to put the five cards in order in his head.

In contrast, when a player looks at the cards very briefly, he has made a good hand. By this point, he knows exactly what he needs to complete his hand – one more of his suit or one more to give him a full house. He doesn't have to stare at the cards very long to figure this out. Because of this, a quick glance at the hand followed by a bet should put you on guard.

Another tell indicating that a player has made a hand is when he wants his friend or spouse to see it. If he shows his hand to the player or stranger next to him, he could simply be sharing his misery at having not made the hand. But if he shows it to his wife or buddy, he probably has something good – he'd rather show them what a good card player he is.

While the tells I've mentioned are common at the low limits, not every low limit player is stupid. Some will try to fool you – they'll do the opposite of what the tell would generally indicate. Despite the occasional actor, these tells are frequently genuine, which is why you must be focusing on the game at all times.

Watching your opponents when you're out of the pot will

allow you to pick up on tells, and that will earn or save you money when you are in the hand.

"You'll Never Beat the Low Limits!"

On some websites I've heard people complain that the low limit games are unbeatable. Some say that the rake is simply too high; others say that there are too many clueless people (fish) playing low limit stud – they stay in with trash and then improve on the river card, which makes the game something of a "crap shoot."

I don't buy these arguments, and neither should you. If a rake is higher than 10%, it *is* too high – but 10% (up to four dollars) has become the standard rake at most card clubs. A card club has to stay in business somehow.

You can also overcome any rake by playing solidly against weaker players – and that's what you will be doing. So many stud players out there are nice people, but they simply have no idea what they are doing. They've played at their kitchen tables for dimes and quarters, and think it's the same thing at the card club, so they call when they shouldn't and stay in hands way too long.

If you study the odds (see the Appendix) and pay attention to your opponents and the cards on the table, you'll have a powerful advantage, and you'll become a good, consistent winner over the long haul.

Do's and Don't's

Here are some of the basics that you need to remember

every time you go to play cards:

- **DO** always remember cards that have been folded.
- **DO** always have a positive attitude.
- **DO** remain focused on your game, even when you're not in the hand.
- **DO** know when to leave when you feel yourself going on tilt.
- **DO** have a general knowledge of the odds so you know when staying in a hand is justified.
- **DO** watch your opponents carefully at all times.

- **DON'T** feel you have to "get even" when you've suffered a bad beat.
- **DON'T** play over your head – play only at the limits you can afford.
- **DON'T** gamble by chasing hands that aren't justified by the odds.
- **DON'T** get overly frustrated by losing a good hand or having a losing session. No one wins all the time – you can do everything right, and still go home with less. In the long run, though, if you stick to what you know, you'll be a winner.

The Last Word

In this book, I've given you solid advice on playing stud poker in the poker rooms at the low limits. What I hope this advice will do is make you a good, consistent winner at seven-card stud poker. There will be times when you will lose – but don't let them bother you. Play your "A" game every time, recall those live cards, know the odds, and remember how to play all the hands we've covered properly, and I'm confident that you can enjoy stud poker more and more. Poker is always fun to play – but it's even more fun when it benefits your wallet. This book will help make that happen.

APPENDIX: THE ODDS

It's important to know the odds in poker. Being math-phobic myself, this sounded difficult when I first started reading about odds. Thankfully, you need not be a math genius to figure out the odds in stud poker. All you have to do is memorize the lists that follow.

As you head to the tables, you'll need to keep a few things in mind. First, these lists will change for the worse when more cards are out – but they do give you a general idea of what the odds are for a given hand, and they help you to determine whether to chase or fold.

Second, these lists are helpful in looking at pot odds. Admittedly, the pot can be rather confusing with a ton of chips stacked in the center in no particular order, but if you have a good estimate of what is in the pot, you can compare the pot odds against the statistical odds for your hand. If the pot is big and giving you very good odds (more value for your bet) you can go ahead and bet, even if looking strictly at the lists would make you fold the hand.

Study these lists and, as I've said, memorize them. They

will help you a great deal as you ponder whether or not you should stick around in a hand or muck it. The lists cover fourth, fifth and sixth streets, going by the different hands that you hold and what your odds are of improving the hands. There's no need to cover third street; it doesn't matter what the odds are of being dealt any three cards. There's also no need to cover seventh street; there are no more cards to come there.

Odds of Making a Full House When You Hold...
Trips on third street: 2 to 1
Trips on fourth street with one odd card: 2.5 to 1
Trips on fifth street with two odd cards: 3.5 to 1
Trips on sixth street with three odd cards: 4 to 1
Two Pair on fourth street: 3.5 to 1
Two Pair on fifth street with one odd card: 5 to 1
Two Pair on sixth street with two odd cards: 10 to 1

Odds of Making a Flush When You Hold...
Three suited cards on third street: 4.5 to 1
Three suited cards and an odd card on fourth street: 8.5 to 1
Three suited cards and two odd cards on fifth street: 23 to 1
Four suited cards on fourth street: 1.25 to 1
Four suited cards and one odd card on fifth street: 2 to 1
Four suited cards and two odd cards on sixth street: 4 to 1

APPENDIX

Odds of Making an Open-Ended Straight When You Hold...
Three to a straight on third street: 4.25 to 1
Three to a straight and one odd card on fourth street: 8 to 1
Three to a straight and two odd cards on fifth street: 22 to 1
Four to a straight on fourth street: 1.5 to 1
Four to a straight and one odd card on fifth street: 2 to 1
Four to a straight and two odd cards on sixth street: 5 to 1

Odds of Making an Inside Straight When You Hold...
Four to a straight on fourth street: 3 to 1
Four to a straight and one odd card on fifth street: 5 to 1
Four to a straight and two odd cards on sixth street: 10.5 to 1

Odds of Making a Single-Ended Straight When You Hold...
Three to a straight on third street: 13 to 1
Three to a straight and one odd card: 25 to 1

These odds help clear up which bets are good and which are just plain idiotic. Perhaps one of the most common mistakes a player makes is when he decides to limp in with several big cards on fifth street, thinking it's okay to do so because three cards are suited. He's forgetting that it's an incredible 23 to 1 shot to make a flush! So, again, memorize these odds or keep them next to you if you play online – they'll help you a great deal in determining when to bet. And remember, these odds get worse as more of your cards are gone, so first and foremost – remember those cards!

GLOSSARY

Action: The betting that occurs in a game. If the game has a lot of action, there is a lot of betting. A game with not a lot of action is tight and passive, with little betting.

All-in: Putting all of your money in the pot.

Ante: The required bet to allow you to play in a hand. The most common ante at the low limits is fifty cents. Many spread-limit games have no required ante at all.

Bad beat: Having a powerful hand get beat by a bigger monster. Spend an hour in a poker room, and you will hear the first of many stories from other players about bad beats they have suffered during play.

Bang away: To bet and raise aggressively to try to build the pot.

Bankroll: Money you have for your poker wagering.

Bet: Putting money in the pot before other players have done so (when it becomes a call or raise).

Bettor: The person who puts the first amount of money in the pot.

Bluff: Placing a bet or raise when you do not believe your hand is the best.

Board: The face up cards on the table in a player's hand.

Boat: Another term for a full house.

Bring-in: A forced bet required of the low card, it can be for a minimum (half of the small bet) or full amount (a full small bet).

Busted draw: A hand that didn't complete.

Buy-in: The amount of chips you start out with. Most card clubs have a minimum buy in for each table that changes as levels increase. Always start out with more than the minimum.

Call: Placing an amount of money in the pot that equals the amount of money that another player has bet.

Calling station: A person who will call most of the time, but not raise or fold.

Cap: Putting the last raise that is allowed in the pot. Frequently three raises are the maximum.

Case: The rank of last card in the deck. An example: you hold two pair, 9s and 5s. A 9 is dead, and you get the last (case) 9.

Cold call: Calling a bet that has been raised.

Check: Not betting anything when the action is to you.

Check-raise: Checking and raising when the action comes back to you.

Chip/Check: The round token used in play of hands. Different colors are used to separate denominations.

Come hand: Having a hand not yet made that has more cards to come. A four-straight on sixth street is an example.

Crack: Beating a hand, usually a big one.

Crying call: Calling with a hand that you do not feel has a good chance to be the winner.

Dog: Slang term for an underdog.

Door card: The first card exposed in a player's hand.

Drawing dead: Drawing to a hand that will not win because another player has already made a larger hand.

Early position: The position of betting when you need to act before most of the other players in the hand. With eight players, early position includes the first three.

Family pot: A pot that involves most of the players at the table.

Fifth street: The fifth card that is dealt to each player.

Fill up: Making a full house.

Fish: An inexperienced player who makes many mistakes and tends to be very loose with his money.

Flush: Five cards that are of the same suit.

Fold: Laying down your cards and dropping out of the hand.

Forced bet: The required bet when you are the low card on third street.

Fourth street: The fourth card that's dealt to each player.

Free card: A card given to each player when every player has checked.

Full house: Holding three cards of the same rank and two of another.

Gut shot: Drawing to an inside straight.

Hole: Those cards that are face down.

Inside straight: A straight that can be made only when a card of one particular rank is dealt. Example: You hold 4 5 7 8. Only a 6 will complete your hand.

Kickers: Your side cards outside of the hand you currently hold. Example: You hold A A Q. The queen is your kicker.

Late position: Being one of the last players to act in a betting round. In a full game of eight players, this is the seventh or eighth spot.

Limit: The amount of money that can be bet on a given round. The limit increases in structured limit games when action gets to fifth street; it's always the same in a spread limit game.

Limp in: Getting to the next round as cheaply as possible by just calling as opposed to raising.

Loose: Playing more hands than are justified by the odds.

Loose game: A game in which most of the players stay in to see hands rather than folding. Loose games tend to have higher pots.

Middle position: Being in the middle of the betting action. With eight players, this includes the fourth, fifth and sixth spots.

Muck: Folding a hand.

Odds: The mathematical probability of achieving a result.

Open-ended straight: A straight that can be made with two cards. Example: You hold 4 5 6 7. A 3 or an 8 will complete your straight.

Open pair: A pair on the board visible for everyone to see.

Outs: Card that will improve the quality of your hand. Example: You have a four-flush, and there are four dead cards. You have five "outs" for your flush.

Pass: Another term for checking.

Pocket: Another way of referring to hole cards.

Pot: The total amount of money wagered in a hand, placed in the center of the table.

Pot odds: Odds calculated by figuring a ratio of the amount of money that is in the pot to the bet you need to call to continue with a hand.

Protecting a hand: Betting aggressively to force other players out who could draw to a bigger hand than what you hold.

GLOSSARY

Quads: Four-of-a-kind.

Rags: Term for lousy cards held by a player.

Raise: Adding money to a bet made by another player.

Rake: The amount of money taken out of each pot by the house.

Reraise: Raising after another opponent has raised.

River: The last card (the seventh) that is dealt face down.

Rolled-up: Three of a kind on the first three cards.

Running cards: Cards that come back-to-back. Example: having a three-flush on fifth street and then catching two of the same suit on sixth and seventh streets to complete your flush.

Sandbag: Playing slowly with a monster hand in an attempt to keep other players in.

Scare card: A card dealt to another player that could indicate a powerful hand being made.

Semi-bluff: Betting with a hand that is not the best but has a chance of improving to the best.

Seventh street: The last card. It is dealt face down.

Set: Another term for three-of-a-kind.

Short-stacked: Playing when you have few chips remaining in front of you.

Side pot: A second pot created when a player goes "all-in." The player going all in has no stake in the side pot.

Sixth street: The sixth card dealt in a hand.

Slowplay: Another term for sandbagging, playing a hand slowly to keep other opponents in to pay you off when you hold a powerful hand.

Stealing the antes: Betting heavily on third street to force all of the other players out so you will win the antes.

Straight: Five cards of different suits in sequence.

Straight flush: Five cards of the same suit in a sequence.

Table stakes: Rule in most games that a player can not take out extra money from his billfold during the course of a hand. This is why a player low on chips must go "all-in" if he does not have enough chips to call a bet or meet the structure requirement.

Tell: Body language by a player that gives clues to what he is holding.

Tip/Toke: A small amount of money given from the pot

winner to the dealer.

Trips: Another term for three-of-a-kind.

Underdog: A hand for which the odds are against its winning.

Under the gun: On third street, it is the player with the low card who is first to act. Later on, it is the player to the immediate left of the player who bets.

Wired pair: A hidden pair in the hole.

NOTES

NOTES

NOTES

Visit our new web site (www.cardozapub.com) or write us for a full list of Cardoza books, advanced and computer strategies.

CARDOZA PUBLISHING

P.O. Box 1500, Cooper Station, New York, NY 10276
Phone (800)577-WINS
email: cardozapub@aol.com
www.cardozapub.com

GREAT POKER BOOKS
ADD THESE TO YOUR LIBRARY - ORDER NOW!

TOURNAMENT POKER by Tom McEvoy - Rated by pros as best book on tournaments ever written, and enthusiastically endorsed by more than 5 world champions, this is a must for every player's library. Packed solid with winning strategies for all 11 games in the World Series of Poker, with extensive discussions of 7-card stud, limit hold'em, pot and no-limit hold'em, Omaha high-low, re-buy, half-half tournaments, satellites, strategies for each stage of tournaments. Big player profiles. 344 pages, paperback, $39.95.

OMAHA HI-LO POKER by Shane Smith - Learn essential winning strategies for beating Omaha high-low; the best starting hands, how to play the flop, turn, and river, how to read the board for both high and low, dangerous draws, and how to win low-limit tournaments. Smith shows the differences between Omaha high-low and hold'em strategies. Includes odds charts, glossary, low-limit tips, strategic ideas. 84 pages, 8 x 11, spiral bound, $17.95.

7-CARD STUD (THE COMPLETE COURSE IN WINNING AT MEDIUM & LOWER LIMITS) by Roy West - Learn the latest strategies for winning at $1-$4 spread-limit up to $10-$20 fixed-limit games. Covers starting hands, 3rd-7th street strategy for playing most hands, overcards, selective aggressiveness, reading hands, secrets of the pros, psychology, more - in a 42 "lesson" informal format. Includes bonus chapter on 7-stud tournament strategy by World Champion Tom McEvoy. 160 pages, paperback, $24.95.

POKER TOURNAMENT TIPS FROM THE PROS by Shane Smith - Essential advice from poker theorists, authors, and tournament winners on the best strategies for winning the big prizes at low-limit re-buy tournaments. Learn the best strategies for each of the four stages of play–opening, middle, late and final–how to avoid 26 potential traps, advice on re-buys, aggressive play, clock-watching, inside moves, top 20 tips for winning tournaments, more. Advice from McEvoy, Caro, Malmuth, Ciaffone, others. 144 pages, paperback, $19.95.

WINNING LOW LIMIT HOLD'EM by Lee Jones - This essential book on playing 1-4, 3-6, and 1-4-8-8 low limit hold'em is packed with insights on winning: pre-flop positional play; playing the flop in all positions with a pair, two pair, trips, overcards, draws, made and nothing hands; turn and river play; how to read the board; avoiding trash hands; using the check-raise; bluffing, stereotypes, much more. Includes quizzes with answers. Terrific book. 176 pages, 5 1/2 x 8 1/2, paperback, $19.95.

WINNING POKER FOR THE SERIOUS PLAYER by Edwin Silberstang - New edition! More than 100 actual examples provide tons of advice on beating 7 Card Stud, Texas Hold 'Em, Draw Poker, Loball, High-Low and more than 10 other variations. Silberstang analyzes the essentials of being a great player; reading tells, analyzing tables, playing position, mastering the art of deception, creating fear at the table. Also, psychological tactics, when to play aggressive or slow play, or fold, expert plays, more. Colorful glossary included. 288 pages, 6 x 9, perfect bound, $16.95.

WINNER'S GUIDE TO TEXAS HOLD 'EM POKER by Ken Warren - This comprehensive book on beating hold 'em shows serious players how to play every hand from every position with every type of flop. Learn the 14 categories of starting hands, the 10 most common hold 'em tells, how to evaluate a game for profit, and more! Over 50,000 copies in print. 256 pages, 5 1/2 x 8 1/2, paperback, $14.95.

KEN WARREN TEACHES TEXAS HOLD 'EM by Ken Warren - In 33 comprehensive yet easy-to-read chapters, you'll learn absolutely everything about the great game of Texas hold 'em poker. You'll learn to play from every position, at every stage of a hand. You'll master a simple but thorough system for keeping records and understanding odds. And you'll gain expert advice on raising, stealing blinds, avoiding tells, playing for jackpots, bluffing, tournament play, and much more. 416 pages, 6 x 9, $24.95.

THE CHAMPIONSHIP BOOKS
POWERFUL BOOKS YOU MUST HAVE

CHAMPIONSHIP OMAHA (Omaha High-Low, Pot-limit Omaha, Limit High Omaha) by T. J. Cloutier & Tom McEvoy. Clearly-written strategies and powerful advice from Cloutier and McEvoy who have won four World Series of Poker titles in Omaha tournaments. Powerful advice shows you how to win at low-limit and high-stakes games, how to play against loose and tight opponents, and the differing strategies for rebuy and freezeout tournaments. Learn the best starting hands, when slowplaying a big hand is dangerous, what danglers are and why winners don't play them, why pot-limit Omaha is the only poker game where you sometimes fold the nuts on the flop and are correct in doing so and overall, how can you win a lot of money at Omaha! 230 pages, photos, illustrations, $39.95.

CHAMPIONSHIP STUD (Seven-Card Stud, Stud 8/or Better and Razz) by Dr. Max Stern, Linda Johnson, and Tom McEvoy. The authors, who have earned millions of dollars in major tournaments and cash games, eight World Series of Poker bracelets and hundreds of other titles in competition against the best players in the world show you the winning strategies for medium-limit side games as well as poker tournaments and a general tournament strategy that is applicable to any form of poker. Includes give-and-take conversations between the authors to give you more than one point of view on how to play poker. 200 pages, hand pictorials, photos. $29.95.

CHAMPIONSHIP HOLD'EM by T. J. Cloutier & Tom McEvoy. Hard-hitting hold'em the way it's played today in both limit cash games and tournaments. Get killer advice on how to win more money in rammin'-jammin' games, kill-pot, jackpot, shorthanded, and other types of cash games. You'll learn the thinking process before the flop, on the flop, on the turn, and at the river with specific suggestions for what to do when good or bad things happen plus 20 illustrated hands with play-by-play analyses. Specific advice for rocks in tight games, weaklings in loose games, experts in solid games, how hand values change in jackpot games, when you should fold, check, raise, reraise, check-raise, slowplay, bluff, and tournament strategies for small buy-in, big buy-in, rebuy, incremental add-on, satellite and big-field major tournaments. Wow! Easy-to-read and conversational, if you want to become a lifelong winner at limit hold'em, you need this book! 320 Pages, Illustrated, Photos. $39.95

CHAMPIONSHIP NO-LIMIT & POT LIMIT HOLD'EM by T. J. Cloutier & Tom McEvoy The definitive guide to winning at two of the world's most exciting poker games! Written by eight time World Champion players T. J. Cloutier (1998 Player of the Year) and Tom McEvoy (the foremost author on tournament strategy) who have won millions of dollars playing no-limit and pot-limit hold'em in cash games and major tournaments around the world. You'll get all the answers here - no holds barred - to your most important questions: How do you get inside your opponents' heads and learn how to beat them at their own game? How can you tell how much to bet, raise, and reraise in no-limit hold'em? When can you bluff? How do you set up your opponents in pot-limit hold'em so that you can win a monster pot? What are the best strategies for winning no-limit and pot-limit tournaments, satellites, and supersatellites? You get rock-solid and inspired advice from two of the most recognizable figures in poker — advice that you can bank on. If you want to become a winning player, a champion, you must have this book. 209 pages, paperback, illustrations, photos. $39.95

POWERFUL POKER SIMULATIONS
A MUST FOR SERIOUS PLAYERS WITH A COMPUTER!
IBM compatibles CD ROM Windows 3.1, 95, and 98 - Full Color Graphics

Play interactive poker against these **incredible** full color poker simulation programs - they're the absolute **best** method to improve game. Computer players act like real players. All games let you set the limits and rake, have fully programmable players, adjustable lineup, stat tracking, and Hand Analyzer for starting hands. MIke Caro, the world's foremost poker theoretician says, "Amazing...A steal for under $500." Includes free telephone support. **New Feature!** - "Smart advisor" gives expert advice for every play in every game!

1. TURBO TEXAS HOLD'EM FOR WINDOWS - $89.95 - Choose which players, how many, 2-10, you want to play, create loose/tight game, control check-raising, bluffing, position, sensitivity to pot odds, more! Also, instant replay, pop-up odds, Professional Advisor, keeps track of play statistics. Free bonus: Hold'em Hand Analyzer analyzes all 169 pocket hands in detail, their win rates under any conditions you set. Caro says this "hold'em software is the most powerful ever created." Great product!

2. TURBO SEVEN-CARD STUD FOR WINDOWS - $89.95 - Create any conditions of play; choose number of players (2-8), bet amounts, fixed or spread limit, bring-in method, tight/loose conditions, position, reaction to board, number of dead cards, stack deck to create special conditions, instant replay. Terrific stat reporting includes analysis of starting cards, 3-D bar charts, graphs. Play interactively, run high speed simulation to test strategies. Hand Analyzer analyzes starting hands in detail. Wow!

3. TURBO OMAHA HIGH-LOW SPLIT FOR WINDOWS - $89.95 -Specify any playing conditions; betting limits, number of raises, blind structures, button position, aggressiveness/passiveness of opponents, number of players (2-10), types of hands dealt, blinds, position, board reaction, specify flop, turn, river cards! Choose opponents, use provided point count or create your own. Statistical reporting, instant replay, pop-up odds, high speed simulation to test strategies, amazing Hand Analyzer, much more!

4. TURBO OMAHA HIGH FOR WINDOWS - $89.95 - Same features as above, but tailored for the Omaha High-only game. Caro says program is "an electrifying research tool...it can clearly be worth thousands of dollars to any serious player. A must for Omaha High players.

5. TURBO 7 STUD 8 OR BETTER - $89.95 - Brand new with all the features you expect from the Wilson Turbo products: the latest artificial intelligence, instant advice and exact odds, play versus 2-7 opponents, enhanced data charts that can be exported or printed, the ability to fold out of turn and immediately go to the next hand, ability to peek at opponents hand, optional warning mode that warns you if a play disagrees with the advisor, and automatic testing mode that can run up to 50 tests unattended. Challenge tough computer players who vary their styles for a truly great poker game.

---

6. TOURNAMENT TEXAS HOLD'EM - $59.95
Set-up for tournament practice and play, this realistic simulation pits you against celebrity look-alikes. Tons of options let you control tournament size with 10 to 300 entrants, select limits, ante, rake, blind structures, freezeouts, number of rebuys and competition level of opponents - average, tough, or toughest. Pop-up status report shows how you're doing vs. the competition. Save tournaments in progress to play again later. Additional feature allows you to quickly finish a folded hand and go on to the next.

GRI'S PROFESSIONAL VIDEO POKER STRATEGY
Win Money at Video Poker! With the Odds!

At last, for the **first time,** and for **serious players only,** the GRI **Professional Video Poker** strategy is released so you too can play to win! **You read it right** - this strategy gives you the **mathematical advantage** over the casino and what's more, it's **easy to learn!**

PROFESSIONAL STRATEGY SHOWS YOU HOW TO WIN WITH THE ODDS - This **powerhouse strategy,** played for **big profits** by an **exclusive** circle of **professionals,** people who make their living at the machines, is now made available to you! You too can win - with the odds - and this **winning strategy** shows you how!

HOW TO PLAY FOR A PROFIT - You'll learn the **key factors** to play on a **pro level:** which machines will turn you a profit, break-even and win rates, hands per hour and average win per hour charts, time value, team play and more! You'll also learn big play strategy, alternate jackpot play, high and low jackpot play and key strategies to follow.

WINNING STRATEGIES FOR ALL MACHINES - This **comprehensive, advanced pro package** not only shows you how to win money at the 8-5 progressives, but also, the **winning strategies** for 10s or better, deuces wild, joker's wild, flat-top, progressive and special options features.

BE A WINNER IN JUST ONE DAY - In just one day, after learning our strategy, you will have the skills to **consistently win money** at video poker - with the odds. The strategies are easy to use under practical casino conditions.

FREE BONUS - PROFESSIONAL PROFIT EXPECTANCY FORMULA ($15 VALUE) - For serious players, we're including this free bonus essay which explains the professional profit expectancy principles of video poker and how to relate them to real dollars and cents in your game.

To order send just $50 by check or money order to:
Cardoza Publishing, P.O. Box 1500, Cooper Station, New York, NY 10276

CARDOZA SCHOOL OF BLACKJACK
- Home Instruction Course - $200 OFF! -

At last, after years of secrecy, the **previously unreleased** lesson plans, strategies and playing tactics formerly available only to members of the Cardoza School of Blackjack are now available to the general public - and at substantial savings. **Now**, you can **learn at home,** and at your own convenience. Like the full course given at the school, the home instruction course goes **step-by-ste**p over the winning concepts. We'll take you from layman to **pro**.

MASTER BLACKJACK - Learn what it takes to be a **master player**. Be a **powerhouse**, play with confidence, impunity, and **with the odds** on your side. Learn to be a **big winner** at blackjack.

MAXIMIZE WINNING SESSIONS - You'll **learn how** to take a good winning session and make a **blockbuster** out of it, but just as important, you'll learn to cut your losses. Learn exactly when to end a session. We cover everything from the psychological and emotional aspects of play to altered playing conditions (through the **eye of profitability**) to protection of big wins. The advice here could be worth **hundreds (or thousands) of dollars** in one session alone. Take our guidelines seriously.

ADVANCED STRATEGIES - You'll learn the latest in advanced winning strategies. Learn about the **ten-factor**, the **ace-factor**, the effects of rules variations, how to protect against dealer blackjacks, the winning strategies for single and multiple deck games and how each affects you, the **true count**, the multiple deck true count variations, and much more. And, of course, you'll receive the full Cardoza Base Count Strategy package.

$200 OFF - LIMITED OFFER - The Cardoza School of Blackjack home instruction course, retailed at $295 (or $895 if taken at the school) is available here for just $95.

DOUBLE BONUS! - **Rush** your order in **now**, for we're also including, **absolutely free**, the 1,000 and 1,500 word essays, "How to Disguise the Fact that You're an Expert", and "How Not to Get Barred". Among other **inside information** contained here, you'll learn about the psychology of the pit bosses, how they spot counters, how to project a losing image, role playing, and other skills to maximize your profit potential.

To order, send $95 (plus postage and handling) by check or money order to:
Cardoza Publishing, P.O. Box 1500, Cooper Station, New York, NY 10276

VIDEOS BY MIKE CARO
THE MAD GENIUS OF POKER

CARO'S PRO POKER TELLS

The long-awaited two-video set is a powerful scientific course on how to use your opponents' gestures, words and body language to read their hands and win all their money. These carefully guarded poker secrets, filmed with 63 poker notables, will revolutionize your game. It reveals when opponents are bluffing, when they aren't, and why. Knowing what your opponent's gestures mean, and protecting them from knowing yours, gives you a huge winning edge. An absolute must buy! $59.95.

CARO'S MAJOR POKER SEMINAR

The legendary "Mad Genius" is at it again, giving poker advice in VHS format. This new tape is based on the inaugural class at Mike Caro University of Poker, Gaming and Life strategy. The material given on this tape is based on many fundamentals introduced in Caro's books, papers, and articles and is prepared in such a way that reinforces concepts old and new. Caro's style is easy-going but intense with key concepts stressed and repeated. This tape will improve your play. 60 Minutes. $24.95.

CARO'S POWER POKER SEMINAR

This powerful video shows you how to win big money using the little-known concepts of world champion players. This advice will be worth thousands of dollars to you every year, even more if you're a big money player! After 15 years of refusing to allow his seminars to be filmed, Caro presents entertaining but serious coverage of his long-guarded secrets. Contains the most profitable poker advice ever put on video. 62 Minutes! $39.95.

DOYLE BRUNSON'S SUPER SYSTEM
A COURSE IN POKER POWER!
by World Champion Doyle Brunson

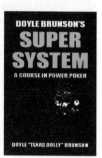